The Graceful Exit

The Graceful Exit

A Pastor's Journey from Good-bye to Hello

Mary C. Lindberg

 | ALBAN

Alban Institute
Herndon, VA
www.alban.org

The Alban Institute
2121 Cooperative Way, Suite 100
Herndon, VA 20171

Unless otherwise noted, all Scripture quotations are from the New Revised Standard Version of the Bible, copyright © 1989, Division of Christian Education of the National Council of the Churches of Christ in the United States of America, and are used by permission.

Library of Congress Cataloging-in-Publication Data

Lindberg, Mary C.
  The graceful exit : a pastor's journey from goodbye to hello / Mary C. Lindberg.
    p. cm.
  Includes bibliographical references (p. 119).
  ISBN 978-1-56699-432-3
  1. Ex-clergy. 2. Vocation, Ecclesiastical. 3. Clergy--Appointment, call, and election. I. Title.
  BV672.5.L56 2012
  253'.2--dc23

                                    2012032977

12   13   14   15   16   VP   5   4   3   2   1

"You should write a book someday," said my mom.
Here it is, Mom . . . for you.

CONTENTS

FOREWORD

You are about to receive a gift. Mary Lindberg has given the church a gift that you the reader will be able to share. If you are a pastor who has made the decision to leave your present call to a ministry of the church, this book will be of enormous help. It will be equally valuable whether you are leaving for a call to a different ministry or you will be without a new call for a while. Many of the issues concerning the ending of a call to a ministry will be the same. For many, the decision will be to retire. *The Graceful Exit* will serve the pastor well as he or she moves into the particularly challenging experience of finding oneself at the end of an active ministry.

If you are a bishop or a member of a judicatory staff who works with pastors and congregations in the call process, either at the beginning or at the ending of a call, *The Graceful Exit* will be an invaluable tool to recommend to pastors and congregations. I was a bishop in both the old American Lutheran Church, Central District and the Rocky Mountain Synod of the Evangelical Lutheran Church in America. How I wish I would have had this resource to share with pastors and congregational leaders. In fact, this book would have helped me a great deal as I left parish calls and particularly when I left the office of the bishop to return to the parish. This type of transition is not so common in the church and that is why this book would have been a very welcome aid to both me and the synod I was leaving.

Mary Lindberg brings to this book years of experience as a parish pastor, a servant in other ministries of the church, and as a mother and wife. This gives her a unique perspective on the process of leaving one call and transitioning into another place of ministry. Her insights on the challenges to the children and spouse of the pastor are most helpful. We often fail to remember that any call is shared with the whole family, which is impacted by our decision to end a call. More attention needs to be paid and more help provided for children and spouses at the time of transition.

You will discover that Mary Lindberg writes very well in clear, often "poetic" prose. She has a wonderful way of creating a catchy or perceptive phrase. I particularly noted, "the concerns of a fraying church and a weeping world" to describe the issues that are always close to the surface for a practicing parish pastor and will not be so central if one leaves parish ministry. You will find that this is a very personal work filled with stories and anecdotes of her own unique journey in ministry.

The Graceful Exit: A Pastor's Journey from Good-bye to Hello is divided into three sections. Part One: The Good Good-bye, Part Two: The Long Good-bye, and Part Three: From Good-bye to Hello. Each section builds on the one before in a logical progression. The author subscribes to the notion that a proper ending is as important as a good beginning when it comes to pastoral ministry. The truth is that if there has not been a good ending, or at least one that has been properly and personally worked through, there cannot be a good beginning. A graceful exit is essential for a gracious and promising beginning to a new ministry. It is as the old song says, "you can't have one without the other."

Each of the major sections is divided into smaller subsections which end with a number of suggestions for reflection. These reflection questions should prove to be one of the most appreciated parts of this book. It actually helps make *The Graceful Exit* into a handbook for almost daily use for the pastor, family, and congregation as a ministry is ending. The author simply assumes that the decision to leave has been made and doesn't dwell on the process of how one comes to the conclusion to end a call. I have discovered an image that may be helpful when one is contemplating whether it is time to end a call and look for another. My experience has shown that a person is often being called away from a ministry he or she is engaged in before feeling called to a new one. There was a professor at the seminary I attended who was quite young in relationship to the student body. He had recently completed a graduate study abroad program and, upon arriving at the school, he began playing softball with the students. He said he knew it was time to quit when he was rounding a base during one game and realized he didn't want to slide! When in the course of a call you find yourself unwilling to go at the ministry with complete commitment and take the attendant risks, it may well be time to consider ending your present call. This works for other vocations as well as the pastoral one. I often used it when talking to legislators about knowing when they had served long enough. To go beyond this is dangerous.

As you continue in your reading of this book, you will discover that Mary Lindberg integrates all she writes into texts of Scripture. The texts of Scripture inform and lead her to conclusions as to what makes an exit graceful. This is one of the most useful features of this work that provides the power and direction for the kind of reflection, action, and integration that makes one's exit graceful. The Holy Spirit will play the key role for anyone who wants to go through an exit from a ministry in a way that will bring both growth and peace. I point you to her use of the Emmaus text in Luke 24 as a clear way the Scriptures can be used to lead us to go where we need to go. You will find many others since the text is full of passages from the Scriptures that will bless us on our way.

Mary Lindberg is obviously a committed "Jesus person," and gives encouragement to center our leaving in an understanding that we want to be continually witnessing to Jesus if our exit is to be truly graceful. Since so much of pastoral ministry centers around our sharing the sacraments of baptism and Eucharist, she makes use of this reality as we consider how to see ourselves in respect to our leaving a call and a particular ministry. Baptism forms a firm basis for our transition out of a pastoral call. She writes, "May you always trust your baptismal call came before your pastoral call."

Mary Lindberg takes very seriously how closely a pastor's personal identity and understanding of who he or she is and his or her worth is tied to being a pastor. When one is no longer serving as a pastor, what then? Who are we? My experience has taught me that this is a very critical piece of reality that must be confronted and dealt with. I vividly remember the tearful anguish of a pastor who was forced to leave active parish ministry because of debilitating cancer. "Who will I be if I am not a pastor?" This man, coming into the pastoral ministry later in life, had found such a feeling of self-worth and purpose for living in being a parish pastor that it was almost too threatening to face the loss of it.

The whole church needs to attend to this often recurring experience of some of its pastors. This takes on deep existential meaning when a pastor has been asked to resign because of sexual misconduct. I had to spend much time with pastors I had to discipline assuring them of the permanence and precedence of their baptismal identity as given them by Jesus Christ.

Congregations should be strongly encouraged to read this book as they play an indispensable role in pastors' comings and goings. For them to be knowledgeable and understanding of the issues raised in this book will help them in their relationship to pastors.

Mary Lindberg writes from her heart and with deep love for the office of the pastoral ministry, the pastors who practice it and the congregations and people who receive and participate in it. She does this with a lightness of touch and good humor. Sometimes humor is the one thing that keeps us from taking beginnings and endings too seriously. I often told this story as I left a call: One of the church's beloved and faithful old members said to her pastor when he announced that he was leaving: "Oh, pastor, you just can't leave us." The pastor replied, "Don't worry, God will send you an even better pastor than me." She retorted, "That is what they all have said and they just keep getting worse and worse."

Wayne Weissenbuehler
Retired bishop now serving as pastor to Faith Lutheran Church in Burlington, Iowa

PREFACE

Twenty girls, ages three to twelve, pile into the entrance of the Korean Cultural Center, where they have come to practice traditional Korean dance. According to Korean custom, everyone takes off their shoes when they enter a building, and the girls observe this ritual—in their own fashion. They topple over one another as they toss their shoes into a large pile and head off to rehearsal. While the dance teacher leads the class, I sit in the lobby, waiting for my daughter and watching another ritual unfold. One of the other moms methodically picks up each of the dozens of shoes in the large pile and sorts them into pairs. She matches up the shoes and sets each pair neatly down, with the toes pointed toward the door. By the end of her ritual she has turned all the shoes around. When our daughters finish dancing, their shoes are ready for them to head out the door and on to the next event in their lives.

Busily engaged in the work of caring for God's people, pastors may not notice anything out of the ordinary about their status in a congregation for a long time. But one day, as a particular awareness dawns or a slight hunch grows stronger, we suddenly realize that God has turned our shoes around. God is helping us get ready to go in a new direction. *Put on your shoes, for this too is holy ground.* Shod once more and heading out that door, pastors will, I hope, pick up this book.

After years of prayer, reams of journal entries, and hours of talks with my spiritual director, I discerned that God had turned my shoes around, and the time had come to leave the parish I had been serving. The process proved to be more significant than I ever imagined for both congregational members and me. I really didn't have a clue what my role as pastor meant to my congregation until I began to leave. I hadn't realized the tensile strength of the bonds that formed over my eight years of ministry there. And in spite of coming to parish ministry via a nonchurch career, I didn't really understand the complexities of moving back to the secular world.

Grieving, realigning, stumbling, church searching . . . all these enterprises filled my time after parish ministry. I had to figure out who I *wasn't* on the way to figuring out who I was. Don't worry—it wasn't all a dour endeavor! Life became humorous as I scaled a steep learning curve of mastering various other occupations. I naively thought I could hang my alb in my closet at home, and my pastoral identity would cling to it, protected by the cleaners' bag that kept it from getting moth-eaten. It turned out that I was wrong about that.

After all the ups and downs and letting go and seeing what's left, I am still a pastor . . . and not just because people gave me that first name or because it's so amazing to serve Communion and baptize babies.

I've shared a call with other pastors to one of the last Renaissance jobs in this world. We have dared to call ourselves God's workers, and God has in turn brought us closer to suffering (even our own) and given us front-row seats to the cosmic battle between good and evil (even our own).

As pastors we share a language and an impossible-to-explain-to-the-world ministry. I don't assume we walk *identical* paths, but I do assume we share a desire to approach our departures from a faith perspective.

Being a pastor is a unique role in this world; so, when we face the grief of saying good-bye to a congregation, the grief will also be a particular form of grief shaped by our role. Some of the unique challenges of our departures have to do with the nature of being a pastor:

> As called and ordained ministers of Christ, we proclaimed our belief in God's words and deeds every Sunday. When we are suddenly home alone, we must ask ourselves, How will we witness to God when we don't stand behind an altar or pulpit?
>
> As trusted clergy, we accompanied so many others through major life events, both literal and figurative births and deaths. After we say good-bye, it is our turn to face loss and change. Who will accompany us?
>
> As church leaders, we worked in a system and culture that is hard to translate in the secular world. Once we move outside a particular congregation, how will we explain ourselves in a world where we can't assume anyone's faith in God?
>
> As worship leaders, we sat in a front-row seat as we worshiped God and practiced Word and Sacrament ministry. How will God look when viewed from a pew?
>
> As constant caregivers, we were distracted and protected by our work from our less-altruistic natures. Who will we be without others to bring out our best?

Two clearly identifiable fears stalked me as I prepared to take a break from parish ministry. I was afraid of (1) losing community and (2) losing purpose. In fact, both of my fears came true, and I resonate with others looking for these underpinnings.

As the daughter of an intuitive listener, as a mom, a pastor, and a spiritual director, I've learned a few lessons about listening. Mostly, that it's hard and holy work. But when I listen, people tell me things. Many insights in this book came from listening to others as they described sorting out their pastor versus nonpastor issues and endured changes in their life work. This book is spawned by my experience, but its value lies in the company that informs, needs, and shares the experience.

I believe in the power of books to ease our way through life's transitions. What helpful book could someone have handed me on the way out the church door? The Bible, of course. Many change themes exist there, including stories of exodus and healing.

In addition to the Bible, I also wanted someone to hand me a guidebook about finding a new church home, about getting a life, about relating to the colleagues who stayed. I wanted a book explaining how to be a pastor in a nonpastoral role. I needed a book about God getting claustrophobic in old boxes that couldn't contain all the possibilities of God. I wanted a book about community to soothe the loneliness of my individualism, a book about how to be graceful in the midst of the awkward unknown. I wanted a book of words to say to God and of answers that others had heard God speak. Ironically, the book I got at the door was a blank journal. St.

Hilary said it this way: "Everything that seems empty is full of the angels of God."[1]

And so it has been.

I hope I have written a book for you that is at least in part the guidebook I needed. You can read this book in whatever order works for you. Each piece stands alone, but my prayer is that you won't stand alone as you read it, but will feel connected to a community of clergy who share a unique and challenging role.

ACKNOWLEDGMENTS

I couldn't have written this book without my editor, Beth Gaede, a wise and loving companion who believed in the purpose of this book and walked the long, holy road with me to bring it home. Thanks to my husband, Chris, and our daughters, Molly and June, who never stopped believing in Mom's project. Thanks to Bob, Susan, and Kelly—who continued to help and hope—and to the pastors and friends who told me their stories and listened to mine.

PART I

The Good Good-bye

After the Prelude

After the prelude
Enrobed in service
It occurs to you
That if they call it an Opening Prayer
There must be a Closing Prayer too
But never mind for now . . .
You chant the *Lord have mercies,*
Proclaim the *Words of God, Words of Life*
And sing the *Hymns of the Day* for days and days
Until enough Amens pile up
And the last chalice is drained
Until it's time for God's rubric:
Go in peace

What Makes a Good Good-bye?

Pastors say good-bye to congregations. Sometimes our good-byes are timely and sweet; sometimes they are jarring and painful. But as we hear the click of the front door of God's house and stand on the sidewalk, we face a unique journey of grief.

In our ministries, we brushed up against holiness; so do we now, in our good-byes. Now we must pull apart the strands of self and role, individual and community. Now we must confront regrets, confusion, and dislocation. Now we must figure out where and who God is at this juncture in our lives.

But before we step out, God invites us in—into Word and Sacrament, into relationships, into our offices, and into our emotions about leaving. Within all these areas we look for answers to the big question we suddenly face: What makes a good good-bye?

As we leave our congregations, we have to discern how to wrap up our era of ministry. We need to figure out how to get out the door without regrets about not having acknowledged the good-bye or not paving the way for the next pastors. Each pastor will define his or her own good good-bye. But as unique as each of our good good-byes may be, we share much in common as pastors at this moment. All of us, in our leave takings, will face spiritual themes of fulfillment, surrender, community, legacy, and separation. We can face them together.

Separation Anxiety

"Each goodbye is a rehearsal for death," mourned Tristram Shandy in Laurence Sterne's famous eighteenth-century novel *The Life and Opinions of Tristam Shandy, Gentleman*. No wonder all of us pastors are nervous about our good-byes. Our robes and stoles can make our good-bye look like a dress rehearsal for death. We'd sooner not read from this script.

Professional actors learn that they must speak one at a time and take care not to step on one another's lines. But at the rehearsal for death entitled "Good-bye to a Pastor," we can easily become so anxious that we overlap the lines of others, rendering us unable to hear them or ourselves.

Someday, back at home after our congregational good-bye, we will be able to perform our own separation and grief soliloquy. But during the weeks and months of pulling apart at church, a whole cast of characters competes to express their sadness, fear, confusion, anger, and relief. Old assumptions raise the anxiety level. What's going on?

- Some parishioners assume that pastors are God's representatives. When we say we're leaving, these folks may feel disbelief and denial. God is not supposed to change!
- Some parishioners fear that a church's entire mission will depart with their pastor. When a congregation "loses" a pastor who helped to enact a vibrant ministry, the grief can be pointed. Who will they be without this leader who loved and led them?

Most congregation members hope that their pastors will be human enough to know how to talk to them about real-life issues, yet godly enough to somehow rise above this world. When pastors say good-bye, we pull back the curtain a little on our interior selves. We reveal that we're very human people with feelings about particular places and ministries.

It's always hard to keep the "I'm just like everyone else" and "I'm set apart for a specific task" aspects of ourselves sorted out. The separation process makes the issue even more pointed. We face a dual challenge as we say good-bye—being both a pastor to our congregation and a friend to ourselves.

Ordination language proclaimed us to be *set apart* as the spiritual leader of a congregation. A congregation called us to lead them through this experience of our departure, just as they called us to shepherd them through other stages in the life of the parish, such as a building project or redevelopment. Leading can be very tricky in this time of change. It's not easy to avoid slogging around in the muck of everyone else's separation anxiety!

As we get ready to go, we're just as prone to be sad, anxious, and scared as our congregation is. So while we're leading them, we're also figuring out how to take care of ourselves and our own separation anxiety. We also need a pastor to take care of our needs. It's tempting to make our parishioners our sounding board for all our emotions—especially because they are so available—but that is unfair and confusing to the people we lead. Our congregation is not our pastor.

We need someone to support us from outside the congregation. Leaving sparks many reactions for us, from joy to distress. We need to find someone with whom we can be open and honest so that our feelings about departure don't bleed all over the people whom we are called to serve. We need someone who has the distance, the perspective on our leaving, to remind us that even a dress rehearsal for death is not death itself. We are not dying; we are leaving. We need someone who is close enough, safe enough, brave enough to walk with us in our intense grieving. We feel an extra-large wallop of despair about losing our job, our congregation, and our colleagues all in one fell swoop, as well as relief, closure, and gratitude for the mission we accomplished together. We need someone, because we can't simultaneously be the chaplain for others' grief and the healer of our own grief. Someone from outside the congregation can help keep us from inadvertently confusing our issues with parishioners' issues. We ultimately want to be there for parishioners but be somewhere else for ourselves.

Yes, each good-bye is a rehearsal for death. We feel your good-bye pain, Tristam Shandy. Saying good-bye to a congregation may be excruciating work. But here's some news for you, Tristam, news that God taught us. Death comes whether or not we rehearse for it, and every death is a rehearsal for life. "For if we have been united with him in a death like his, we will certainly be united with him in a resurrection like his" (Rom. 6:5).

For Reflection . . .

1. What scares you most about separating from parishioners?
2. What feelings keep coming up that are asking you to pay attention?
3. Write a conversation between yourself and Death.
4. Practice explaining your understanding of death to several people. First, imagine how you would talk about death with a senior citizen, then with a middle-aged person, then with a teenager, and finally with a child.

The Graceful Exit: Anna and Simeon

Pastors started "texting" long before the rest of the world caught on. Ever since God's people began to pass on stories and messages about God's work among them, faith leaders have leaned on texts to tie them to God and God's people.

All around us, modern day texters gaze down at palm-sized gadgets and press tiny keyboards with their thumbs. Because sending a text message is cumbersome, texters use as few words and symbols as possible to communicate the crux of their message. We pastors also work to condense biblical texts down to their core, but for a different reason. Our purpose is to help both our listeners and ourselves focus on what's essential. I recall reading Christian educator Maria Montessori's words that there's a road into a text, and our job is to find it. The Bible texting that we've practiced throughout our ministry has led us and our communities down those roads to God's truths.

Thanks to the texting craze, thumbs in every part of the world have never been so fit. People are using their thumbs all day long to do what humans have *always* longed to do, connect with one another. Pastors understand that desire. But the goal of our pastoral practice of biblical texting is not about speed, like the rest of the world's texting, even though we do often hope that God would get back to us quickly. Our goal is not to text God with our thumbs but with our souls. We commit ourselves to scriptural texts, because we also long to connect—with God and God's people. We "text" the Bible as fervently as teenagers text their friends, hoping to receive answers to our questions: What does God want us to see and hear in the texts? How did God's people in that bygone era attempt to live faithfully?

Every year at church, as we methodically text through Jesus's life, death, and resurrection in the lectionary cycle, the Bible slowly but surely unveils new pictures of God and shakes up old *text-pectations.*

God's Word, delivered as biblical texts, offers *con-text*. Context allows us to place all kinds of events, including our departure, within God's larger story of salvation history. As we leaf through the Bible, we rediscover that God called people to move on again and again. God repeatedly expected people to get going—away from old sins, onto water, across barriers, out of exile, behind a Savior, into a Spirit-filled unknown.

And when God's people do get going, they learn new lessons. Departures and revelations are intimately tied together in the Bible, as we see, for example, in the story of Anna and Simeon.

Sometime between making the decision to leave our congregation and announcing our news to the community, we need to make a visit. Undoubtedly, we need to make lots of visits, but this particular visit should rise to the top of the list. We need to go see Anna and Simeon, two biblical mentors who can teach us about leaving gracefully. They remind us that our endings are about Jesus, not just us; they teach us that our departures fit into much bigger stories; and they model the language of good-bye, a prayer-filled language of proclamation and thanksgiving.

Luke 2:25–38 recounts the story of a God-fearing elder named Simeon and an eighty-four-year-old prophetess named Anna. God's promises had sustained Simeon and Anna as they waited and waited for Jesus, the promised Messiah. The Holy Spirit had prophesied that Simeon would depart this world as Jesus entered it, and Simeon trusted that his life would be complete—and completed—when he saw God's Son. Finally notified by the Holy Spirit that God's time was ripe, Simeon traveled to the temple and found baby Jesus there, along with

Mary and Joseph. He reached for the baby and cradled Jesus in his arms. Then Simeon spoke poetry to the assembly— "For my eyes have seen your salvation"—and prophesied to Mary and Joseph that all lives would be shaped by the power of this child.

Anna had spent her widowed existence in the temple (like some of our church regulars!). Like Simeon, she had kept her waiting eyes focused on a vision of God's Son. She had firmly placed herself in a posture of readiness for Jesus's arrival, so when Mary and Joseph presented their son, she joined Simeon "at that moment." A lifetime of spiritual richness—and a baby—centered Anna and Simeon as they waited for their moment and carried out their part of God's story.

In the end, after waiting, holding baby Jesus, and witnessing to his power, Simeon and Anna left the scene. Their work of beholding and sharing Jesus was complete. Mary and Joseph packed up their Messiah baby and set off for Nazareth. Now the time had arrived for Simeon and Anna to exit the story— their lines delivered, their faith passed on. God's Holy Spirit held Anna and Simeon by the elbow and accompanied them to another unseen place in God's story, and so they walked out of the temple, off the page, and into our lives. Now they hold our elbow and suggest to us some ways of going gracefully as we step out of our parish.

PASS JESUS AROUND AS YOU SAY GOOD-BYE

Anna and Simeon held on to Jesus with their prayers and hope, while God's Spirit held onto them in love. Finally, their vision of Jesus had become incarnate, and Simeon got to hold baby Jesus. But Simeon didn't try to keep Jesus for himself and take Jesus out the door with him. Instead, Simeon passed baby Jesus to Anna. And Anna passed Jesus on to everyone who longed to hold him: "At that moment she came, and began to praise God and to speak about the child to all who were looking for the redemption of Jerusalem" (Luke 2:38).

African women can teach us much about passing babies around. Every Sunday morning at worship services in Tcholliere, Cameroon, West Africa, women practice a weekly ritual of passing their babies around during worship. Babies get plenty sleepy, hungry, and fussy during worship services that last two to three hours. So the churchwomen pass their babies down the rows, across the aisles, even in and out of the open doors to the crowds listening outside. When one woman can't comfort a crying baby, the child is passed to another woman to rock her and pat her back. When a squirmy baby gets antsy in one pew, he is passed overhead to another pew, where women bounce him on their knees and kiss his little head. Even sleeping babies are shared, so that more than one woman gets to feel the calm of a sweet slumbering bundle. Cameroonian churchwomen know that many different churchwomen have gifts to offer each baby and that each woman needs to express her love.

As we begin to say good-bye, we get the chance to follow the lead of Simeon, Anna, and the Cameroonian churchwomen: God calls us as Christian leaders to pass Jesus around as we say good-bye. What does that mean? I think that passing Jesus around means sharing our devotion, not being afraid to talk about Jesus and how God helps us through the person of Jesus. Passing Jesus around also means remembering that no one holds the market on faith in Jesus Christ. We may all

practice our faith a little differently, just like we all say good-
bye a little differently. But we can all feel equally sincere about
what we believe, and God hears all our prayers.

TRUST THAT ENDINGS TIE US TOGETHER, EVEN AS THEY PULL US APART

Anna and Simeon believed that God delivered a promise of
fulfillment and salvation to all people, not only to the two of
them, and Simeon's words continue to tie him to God's people.
"For my eyes have seen your salvation, and the glory of your
people Israel." *Nunc dimittis* are the Latin words for the first
phrase of Simeon's recitation, and for centuries, Christians
have sung the Nunc Dimittis after we share in Communion,
after we have passed around Jesus.

Every Sunday we, along with Simeon, have been practicing our good-byes to one another. God's people of Israel
awaited Jesus throughout salvation history. Countless generations of God's folks arrived and departed before and after
Jesus's appearance. We are tied to all those people, even if we
feel alone when we walk out the door. Our good-byes tie us
to the infinite number of other good-byes that God noticed
and used for God's redemption.

Anna and Simeon show us that our good-byes do not
merely belong to us; our good-byes belong to communities that also shared our hellos and the time between hello
and good-bye. Anna's good-bye was set in the context of a
larger community of God's people. The Bible names Anna
as a daughter of Phanuel from the tribe of Asher. Simeon
announced his good-bye to a gathered assembly, not over his
shoulder as he was slinking off alone. We share our good-byes

with many others—our congregational families as well as our friends, spouses, and children. We share our finitude with all humanity.

Apparently God's plan all along was that endings would be part of life for God's people. Simeon didn't get to stay with Jesus and watch him grow. As relationships change and we grow older, we finally begin to see what Jesus means for the world, and then we face the pain of walking away, of separation from beloved communities. But God shows us that endings can actually fulfill promises. Simeon and Anna waited their whole lives, trusting in God's promises. Why could they go out the door gracefully? Because God kept the promise that sustained so many people. Because this sighting of God carried Anna and Simeon, and those who surrounded them, all the way to the next sighting.

CHECK FOR GOD AT YOUR ELBOW

God didn't spare Simeon and Anna from the pain of saying good-bye, but their good-bye was eased by God's presence. God showed up in the story of Anna and Simeon—in the temple, in worship, in Jesus, in the Holy Spirit. Anna and Simeon responded to God's presence with prayers of wonder and thanks.

Anna knew prayer. She spent her days in prayer at the temple. She grounded herself in speaking and listening to God. When Anna saw Jesus, she responded with thanks, another prayer.

Simeon offered a prayer of his own: "Master, now you are dismissing your servant in peace." Peace can be hard to come by in many departures. Simeon reminds us that we can ask for it.

God honored Anna and Simeon with a promise that
they would encounter God and a glimpse of God's salvation. When they finally saw Jesus, these two faithful elders
gracefully surrendered to the call of departure. "Now let your
servant go in peace, according to your word." They waved
their graceful good-bye, acknowledging that life has beginnings, middles, and endings.

May we find what they asked for, "a light for revelation
to the Gentiles."

For Reflection . . .

1. What were you waiting for during your pastorate?
2. How have God's promises been fulfilled during your
   era of pastoral ministry?
3. The spiritual life is more often circular than linear.
   Download a finger labyrinth at http://www.
   labyrinths.org (click on "Resources"). As you "walk"
   the labyrinth, you can contemplate the places where
   you waited for God, and where God waited for
   you, during your ministry. Write about what you
   discovered.
4. What were the most graceful parts of your ministry?
   We can continue to employ our graceful gifts of God
   during the days and weeks of saying good-bye.

Dear Body of Christ

We sojourned to the temple with Anna and Simeon; we
climbed the stairs to the upper room with Jesus and his disciples. We have texted; we have tasted. Now it's time to tell.

After ten years in his parish, Pastor Dale felt the rhythm of parish ministries running smoothly and parishioners working together for positive causes. He had worked hard to get to this place. He had fostered lay leadership and learned from his mistakes. His congregation had trusted and treasured Pastor Dale, so Pastor Dale's nagging sense that he needed to leave tied him up in knots.

Pastor Dale's wife had recently lost her job, and the two of them had always spoken of their dream of taking a year off to travel the world. Was this the moment? Pastor Dale mulled over his decision ad nauseam. Part of his quandary occurred because he was trying to make two decisions at once: (1) whether to say good-bye to a particular congregation and (2) whether he should say good-bye to parish ministry forever. Pastor Dale felt comfortable in a collar, but he also felt weary of the sacrifices inherent in being a pastor. By combining his two decisions, Pastor Dale caused himself additional distress and found it even harder to come to a resolution.

In fact, Pastor Dale had to make only one decision—whether to leave this parish. If he decided to leave and travel, Pastor Dale would meet God on one continent after another and perhaps find the perspective he needed to make the "should I be a pastor some more" decision.

But even a one-part ministry decision can be brutal. Pastor Dale's angst about leaving stemmed from the strong relationships he'd built in his congregation. He worried about whether the church would continue to thrive, how he would be able to let go of the people he loved, and whether it was okay to desire new ways of serving God.

So . . . Pastor Dale paid attention to his discernment work. He talked as honestly as he knew how—with his wife, with a mentor, with other pastors—about the Spirit moving within him. He tried to be realistic about what he could lose that he could never replace. Pastor Dale knew either decision would include sacrifices and costs, but his nagging sense of wanting to go didn't disappear—and he decided to make the break.

Somewhere deep inside, Pastor Dale believed that traveling the world for a year would make him a wiser and more aware pastor. It was just . . . that "saying good-bye" thing!

Pastors frequently need to write as part of their jobs—sermons, newsletter articles, website copy, and so forth. But few writing assignments carry as much weight as composing a resignation letter.

How many stamps do we need to put on a resignation letter? Pastor Dale had to weigh one and feel the weight of all that a resignation letter tries to accomplish.

- A resignation letter invites us to clarify our reasons for leaving, even if only to ourselves.
- A resignation letter contains the words we can see as well as the questions between the lines. Will they forgive me? Is it possible to love the people but not the job?
- A resignation letter turns our internal process into an external announcement. Our ambiguity, distress, or sense of a new call is no longer private or deniable.
- A resignation letter, once published, unleashes myriad reactions from parishioners that can add to our own ambiguity.
- A resignation letter uncovers many of our feelings about leaving. We literally see our certainties and our vulnerabilities as we notice whether we slow down or speed up as we write each word.

Given the heft of the meaning attached to a resignation letter, Pastor Dale decided to write two versions of his letter of resignation—and he made sure not to get them mixed up! First, at a place away from church, he handwrote the letter he really wished he could send. He bravely wrote the truth, in all its ambiguity:

> I am immensely relieved to leave; I'm terrified to leave; I'm heartbroken to leave. This is what you mean to me. This is what the gospel means to me.

Finding words for his feelings and beliefs was a relief in itself.

As he composed his first letter, Pastor Dale realized that he was also writing to God. "We try to hold so much in our souls, and our souls get filled to overflowing," thought Pastor Dale. His letter became a prayer of thanks, confession, and supplication. And truly, Pastor Dale's first letter became his backstory, the unseen structure of feeling and faith that supported his words as he typed his second letter, the official letter of resignation. This step proved so much easier, because he wasn't working so hard to avoid saying what he'd said in the first letter. He had already gotten those feelings out. Finally, Pastor Dale read the second letter out loud so that he could hear whether it conveyed his care for his congregation. He amended it, drawing on the tone in parts of his first letter, and ultimately felt satisfied with the professional and pastoral result.

After Pastor Dale had reread his letter aloud so many times that he had practically memorized it, he surrendered it to the church council president—who later carried to the post office the stuffed and stamped envelopes addressed to the congregation's members.

Pastor Dale mentally followed his resignation letter to many mailboxes. He tried to imagine the reaction of each parishioner who read the letter. He assumed that many people would be surprised and loved ones would be let down. He recognized that as much as we pastors make our own decisions, we are also public servants, vulnerable to public opinion. While Pastor Dale waited for the letters to go out into the world of his congregation, he continued to write for himself:

> They don't come to church because of me; they come to church because of God. Can you love the people and not the job? It's essential that I tell this community that I love them. Start there. Will they forgive me? That's the fear that's haunting me. If I can keep pointing beyond myself, it should help others do the same. Just let me face my fifteen minutes of unwanted fame and get on with it.

Even after mailing the letter and feeling the release of a decision made, Pastor Dale still invited his doubts in for tea while he waited for the fallout. *On the one hand, I'm relieved*, he thought. *On the other hand, I'm grieved.* Two hands. He turned up his palms and studied his hands. The same two hands that he lay on people's heads for healing services, the same hands that held and splashed water on a baby. The two hands that God gave him.

Pastor Dale held his breath while he felt the Spirit's breath on his two hands. The members of his congregation felt surprised and dismayed when they first read his news. Getting over that initial hurdle took weeks for the congregation as well as for Pastor Dale. For the first time in a long time, the community grappled with the reality that they were going in a different direction than their pastor. In the end, Pastor Dale also felt surprised—by the outpouring of love he received at church on the first Sunday after he sent his resignation letter. His two hands clasped other hands at the door, and when he arrived home, he wrote about that day.

> My life doesn't belong to me. For all my whining and angst and internal discernment, I was part of something much bigger than I realized. They saw me as part of something much bigger than my little life. In the midst of my confusion, they still saw me as their spiritual leader. And they had expectations of me. To love them. You know what? Whatever I did or didn't accomplish, I did love them.
>
> To see God uncovered so profoundly in a community makes me dread a life without that connection. Where and when and how will I find it next? So much of this happened because I finally listened to God and resigned. I've been so amazed at how that move has opened things up in my relationships—family, colleagues, parishioners. I wouldn't have known this freedom without mine. We live alone and in community.

During his final days at the church, Pastor Dale kept a Bible, a world atlas, and a journal on his desk. Pastor Dale rediscovered the story in Genesis of God calling Sarah and Abraham to head out. He flipped through the pages in his atlas. Words and countries swam before Pastor Dale, hints of what he couldn't possibly know until he departed, and arrived.

For Reflection . . .

1. What do you think a letter of departure needs to convey?
2. What letters and messages have you received that carried important news? Consider how those writers presented what they had to say.
3. Try Pastor Dale's technique: Write a first letter about your departure for yourself and another for your congregation.

Packing and Unpacking

When we leave our congregations, we face a dual task— packing up the possessions that we can see and unpacking the feelings inside us that we assume no one can see.

OUR LIFE IN BOXES

Packing up our office affords a concrete task in the midst of nebulous and myriad feelings about leaving.

Packing Offers Calm at the Center of the Leaving Storm

Feelings about our departure swirl around. Everyone seems to have an opinion, an emotion, a comment, or a question. Amid the waves of tasks and feelings crashing around us, the books, papers, office supplies, art, and knickknacks we need to go through and pack offer us something tangible to touch. Attending to the possessions we will be taking away gives us some personal time and offers an opportunity to focus and reflect.

As we head to the sacristy to pick up our robes and stoles, we can sit down in a pew and take some time with God. As we go through old pictures, we can treasure church relationships. As we go through old sermon files, we can remember how God's Word surprised and blessed us.

Packing Disassembles a Life

With every book and file that we store in a box, we drive home the truth that we are disassembling our old life. Our books, little homes for big ideas, will not sit on our shelves in exactly these places. What used to be *in place* will now be out of place. The habits and structures of utility that we figured out (pastoral care books on second shelf right, church council minutes in file cabinet left) will be retired, at least temporarily. A mystery echoes after we take apart our former life: Go where you're called, but don't assume you can carry it all out. Some parts of you will always remain.

Packing Reminds Us of What We Did—and Didn't Do

Reviewing the materials in the piles and drawers reminds us of the abundant life we witnessed over our years in a congregation. Our old files, bulletins, and mementos—the Bobblehead Luther from our confirmation class, the hand-drawn pictures that kids drew during our sermons, a drawer full of business cards—give us a chance to recall innumerable experiences. As we view our accumulation, we ponder: Was the ministry that happened in this congregation close to the ministry we envisioned?

We pull down our diplomas and ordination certificate from the walls and try to remember: What were the ordination promises we made? We might not remember promising to leave when the time was ripe, but caring for others by letting go can be powerful. We definitely promised to practice Word and Sacrament ministry and to care for God's people. But Jesus didn't imagine that we needed all this stuff to do so. "Cure the sick, raise the dead, cleanse the lepers, cast out demons. . . . Take no gold, or silver, or copper in your belts, no bag for your journey" (Matt. 10:8–10). If we followed Jesus's instructions, we wouldn't have anything to pack up, would we? But we didn't work on the road like Jesus; we worked at a desk—a desk where words arrived, where piles and projects overlapped, where calls came in.

As we pack up, we can get down on our knees and look under our desk to check this out: How deep are the indentations in the carpet from the legs of our desk? They remind us of the ruts we got into in our ministries. Perhaps we needed to turn things around more often and get a new perspective. As long as we're on our knees anyway, we might as well pray for broader visions in our future ministry.

Our offices not only contain packable items, they also hold experiences we carry away only in our memories. Our offices often served as the places where we planned how to do God's work and care for God's people. Our offices became sanctuaries for several people who came to talk to us. The prayers of the people paper the walls of our office. Sacredness lingers in the tears that spilled on the armrests, the feet that shuffled under a chair.

So we pack up, look around, and entrust our sacred office spaces to the next pastor. Our pastoral ministry belongs to God, not to us and not to just one congregation. And our office belongs to a congregation, not to just one pastor. Our office belongs to the *office* of pastor. After all our accoutrements get stripped away—and our office looks as bare as the altar at the close of Maundy Thursday—the mandate remains for us and for whoever occupies this space: Love one another.

Our Life Out of the Box

Meanwhile, in the midst of all that stowing of our stuff, we face another challenge: being honest with ourselves about the feelings roiling around inside us.

Why not just stow our feelings about our transition in more boxes? Because sharing our real emotions releases them and keeps them from weighing us down. The truth connects us to others and uncovers clues for our next steps.

Uncertainty

As I was making the decision about whether to leave the parish I'd been serving, I met with a respected colleague who understood the world of pastors. He asked me about my plans for the future, and I stammered about this and that. Truthfully, I looked forward to staying home with our children and writing on a freelance basis, but that didn't exactly sound like a *plan*.

My colleague listened carefully. Then he said something I never forgot: "God doesn't call us to a vacuum."

Perhaps that sound bite from our conversation has stuck with me because I don't think I agree with it. If God doesn't call us to a vacuum, then what about all the seekers who have faced emptiness on their spiritual journeys? Wasn't the wilderness a vacuum for Jesus? God called him there.

Still, I worried that my lack of a call to another formal ministry setting could be a vacuum. The fear of the unknown certainly haunted me. I gave up lots of security to follow what I thought I heard from God. Did I hear incorrectly? A vacuum sounded dangerously worthless. What if I got stuck there?

In spite of my conversation with my colleague and my questions, I felt pretty clear I was being called away from my congregation by God, even if I was hoping that God didn't mess up this one time and accidentally call me to a vacuum. As it worked out, many days at home I felt like I'd been called to a vacuum cleaner!

My prayer to God during the years of discernment finally crystallized into this prayer: "God, please give me the courage to either stay or go." The courage to go didn't arrive in a big package one day. Instead, that courage accumulated over years, so I didn't doubt the authenticity of my decision. But the whole vacuum question did haunt me a bit. Would the vacuum suck me into a godless place? Would God still love me and give me purpose if I weren't a pastor?

In the months after my departure, I definitely faced days of aimlessness, but now, years later, I don't feel that I was stuck in wasted time or a vacuum. God called our family to a new church community. God called me to many writing projects, including this book.

Awkwardness

We're all supposed to want our fifteen minutes of fame, right? Wrong. I tired of my church "fame" long before it was over. Don't get me wrong . . . I need attention as much as the next pastor. I wanted congregation members to pay attention to me when I preached and taught classes.

But life at church felt much more awkward when the attention I received was about my resignation. "What will you do next? Are you still going to go to church here?" I answered those questions dozens of times. And they were not easy questions, given that I wasn't leaving to serve another congregation. That attention seemed to go on for a long time as more and more people heard the news. It felt weird to be the topic of conversation and speculation. I suppose if we all go through that under-the-microscope experience once in a while, we understand how others feel when they are suddenly thrust into the limelight.

Parishioners shared with me many responses to my news. I'll always remember the beloved parishioner who couldn't say a word the Sunday after he received my resignation letter; he just gave me a big hug. Or the young man who seemed inspired, rather than shocked or dismayed, by my decision. "Good for you for taking a risk," he said. Then there were the parishioners who chose to let someone else own their feelings: "Your leaving will be so hard for the children!" they told me. The children, in fact, lived in the moment. Most of them didn't feel a need to say good-bye until my last day.

Once we pastors have made, and announced, the deci-sion to leave, we must all deal with new realities. The people around us in the congregation can't pretend that any of us are immune to change, nor can they pretend that their pastor was 100 percent content in the congregation. As parishioners let go of us as their pastor, they may need to focus on our humanness. It's easier to say to good-bye to a flawed individual.

Sadness

On the Tuesday after my last Easter in the parish, I wandered into the sanctuary looking for some props our kids had used during an Easter Vigil play. Maybe the smell of the Easter lilies that still stood around the altar caught me off guard. Maybe the suddenly quiet space invited me to linger. Without planning to do so, I sat down in the front pew—and began to sob.

My tears poured down before any thoughts could catch up and explain them. I had no idea that the well of sadness inside me was so deep—and so wet! In that moment I knew again how privileged I was to be a pastor in a congregation. I cried about the good-byes and the loss of my role. I cried because it was so darn beautiful and wonderful in that place. I cried because I was leaving my church home and I had no idea where the next home would be. I cried because I am God's child, and I got to express my love for God by being a pastor. In that moment it hit me that I wasn't going to unmake my decision. I was walking away from something I loved. God met me in that front pew. God knew the power of a place and the anguish of trust.

It's hard to imagine how much you have been fed by all those pictures kids give you that they drew in church and all those conversations with new parents and all the smiles you see when you are processing down a church aisle—until you're home alone, missing the connections.

Relief

Along with sad and awkward feelings came the sense that I was doing what I had prayed God would lead me to do. Guilt flirted with me during my leave taking, but I didn't submit to guilt's wiles. I had done my spiritual work of praying, writing, talking, and taking a risk. So even though the walking away hurt a lot, and I felt the same moments of doubt we all feel when we change our life and many other lives, God gave me an immense well of peace to draw from about my decision to leave. My relief was right in there with my sadness and discomfort.

Leaving any job brings some sense of relief. We can finally be done with the parts of the jobs we detested. I wasn't at all sorry I would not have to find any more Sunday school teachers. And as an introvert, I was ready to quit being a public figure for a while. I was built for preaching, listening, and teaching, but years of meeting more and more strangers and leading large public events had drained me.

Still, I was naively surprised by the enormity of the leaving process for all of us. Saying good-bye to a pastor is not just, "See ya!" Congregations may use or misuse their leaders, just as leaders may use or misuse their congregations. But we are tied in a unique relationship that does not end without anyone noticing. I knew I cherished my relationships in the church, especially with my co-pastors, but I failed to understand what I meant to so many parishioners as a pastor, not only as a person. My role as children-and-family pastor meant that parents had a partner with whom to share their deep desire to pass on the faith to their children.

What did I mean to the parishioners? I can begin to imagine the answer to that question now as I recognize what my pastor means to me. I realized what she means to me at a recent baptism of three-year-old and five-year-old sisters. When my pastor gently placed those little girls' hands on the edge of the baptismal font, and when she carefully lifted them back down after their baptisms, I sat in awe. I looked at my pastor's hands and saw the strength there. She rocked that baptism! She talked to the kids about water, and we all listened. She loved those little girls as she spoke of God's love.

I believe that's why my parishioners loved me. I stepped into my faith, and they stepped into theirs. They trusted me to tolerate, teach, inspire, and get to know their children. Along the way we shared conversations, vulnerabilities, and deep desires. My parishioners saw me being a mom to our daughters, and I shared my children with them as they shared theirs with me. They missed me because I tried to be myself, and because I enjoyed dreaming up engaging ways to teach Bible school and first communion.

When I think of my pastor retiring in a year or two, I feel a scary emptiness inside me. That must have been how my parishioners felt. We shared moments you don't share with many people in this world. All of us may have several friends, acquaintances, and colleagues—but we have only a few pastors. We trust our pastors to live their faith, to keep our confidences, to be there when we are in despair and joy. We count on our pastors to carry out a grueling job that can only be done with God in the picture.

I loved being loved like I was as a pastor. I sensed that people loved my role as much they loved me. I could be their spiritual leader, something we all need. I loved the little hands that found mine during Children's Time, the honest secrets that people shared with me, the rush of digging deep to pull off Bible school week. All those moments and people filled and shaped me. Both pastors and parishioners invest themselves in the congregation and their relationships with one another. These relationships can bless both pastors and parishioners.

I left with both tears and smiles adorning my departure day as we celebrated great memories and positive relationships. We laughed about shared moments and prayed each other into an unknown but much hoped for future.

For Reflection . . .

1. As you were packing up, what did you discover on that dusty top shelf that made you wish you could stay?
2. What were you glad to get rid of, pass on to someone else, or leave behind?
3. What experiences in this congregation changed the way you do ministry?
4. Write a letter of welcome to the next pastor and leave it on your desk.

Good-bye, Oprah-Style

When Oprah said good-bye after twenty-five years as a talk-show host, the whole world heard the news. Oprah capitalized on her impending departure by naming her final season her "farewell season." I wonder what a farewell season would look like for a pastor in a congregation. Perhaps we could line up old confirmation photos so that we could see how our glasses changed or our hairlines receded over the years. Or we could count down to our final Sunday.

Even if the end scared her, Oprah was proactive about her good-bye. She amassed the Band-Aids and ibuprofen: this *is* going to hurt. Talking about her impending departure and sharing her mix of emotions undoubtedly was part of a plan to boost the ratings during her farewell season. But Oprah didn't get through twenty-five years of public life without being authentic. You could hear the genuine tone in Oprah's voice when she asked the former talk-show hosts whom she brought together for a reunion, "What is it like the last time you walk off the stage?"

Weeks and months ahead of time, Oprah was getting ready for that day when her show would actually be over. She was dealing with anticipatory grief—that's what we call her strategy in pastoral care language. Anticipatory grief can be very helpful; you can sort of dose out your sadness into manageable quantities. And anticipatory grief is practical; you have time to state your wishes and to divide up what you will leave behind.

But anticipatory grief has its downside. If endings are like cold lakes, anticipatory grief is like trying to get used to the water incrementally. We reason that if we enter the water slowly enough, we can avoid the freezing pain and shock of the cold. Unfortunately, even after our feet and thighs and belly stop being shocked and numbed by the water, more adjustments loom. We haven't eliminated that final, necessary motion: diving under and becoming completely drenched. No matter how many square inches of our skin adjust to the water temperature, we still have to endure a shock at the end, a moment of surrender. Only then can we quit standing on the bottom and begin to swim.

Oprah's leaving lesson for us pastors? Give stuff away! But we don't have cars and vacations and free bridal gowns to offer, like Oprah did. What do we have to give away? Extra forgiveness? Bonuses of grace? Extra large chunks of Communion bread? I'm not thinking of those gifts! But we too can look in our larder of abundance and feel the swell of generosity. We may find little crosses from Lent in our desk, junk to us but treasures to a five-year-old Sunday schooler. We may find several stoles in the sacristy that a young, up-and-coming pastor could not afford. We could even give away a trip to the Holy Land. No, not a real trip—but a darn good read. Bruce Feiler's *Walking the Bible* is a great book and DVD. And then there are our reflections of gratitude and wonder, perhaps saved up until the end, that we can distribute in newsletters and on our blog. One pastor combed through seventeen years' worth of newsletter articles and pulled together a "best of" collection organized according to the church year. He went to an office supply store and had spiral-bound copies made to give away. We can also shower the congregation with prayer in our final season, applying a daily discipline of holding our people in God's light.

Long before Oprah thought of the idea, Jesus taught us to give things away when we leave. Jesus shopped for parting gifts for his disciples when he was on the way to the cross. He found three promises to share: First, Jesus promised to make a home in his disciples' hearts (John 14:23). Second, Jesus promised to fill the disciples with a spirit of courage and comfort. "The Holy Spirit . . . will teach you everything, and remind you of all that I have said to you" (John 14:26). Finally, Jesus promised to sustain his disciples with a special kind of peace. "Peace I leave with you; my peace I give to you" (John 14:27). A home, courage, and peace. Those sound even better than a car!

Like Oprah, we're leaving. We can learn from her openness about her departure, her anticipatory grief, and her generosity of spirit. Oprah didn't know who would *replace* her anymore than we may know the next pastor who will sit in *our* chair. So we'll open the gifts Jesus gave us—a home in him, the courage to move on, the peace that will get us through many unknowns. And we'll trust that God is staying with those we love for many more seasons.

For Reflection . . .

1. When have you witnessed parishioners' anticipatory grief?
2. What does gift giving mean in your family or culture?
3. At what times have you received the gift of Christ's peace during the process of leaving?
4. Make a list of ten items from your ministry that you would be willing to give away, and possible recipients.

Making the Good-bye
Good for Our Families

We teach our kids to call a church building God's house, but I underestimated the impact leaving her congregational home would have on our ten-year-old daughter. I didn't realize how much she identified with her church.

When she found out we were leaving our congregation, our ten-year-old felt both sad and outraged. It felt great to be the pastor's kid when she was loved by all and got sneak previews of Bible school activities. It hurt to be the pastor's kid when Pastor Mom left her job and she lost her church home.

Like all overprotective parents, we thought it our duty to tell our ten-year-old about the upcoming change as soon as we decided. This happened to be a couple of months ahead of my actual departure date. In retrospect, I can see that this was a mistake. We expected her to keep her feelings a secret from some of the people she loved dearly. That's too much to ask of a ten-year-old. She was getting ready to move away from home, yet the people with whom she shared that home didn't know about it.

Our daughter's internal confusion about the secret she was keeping literally spilled over at a children's choir concert at church. The beauty of the music matched the glow of the children's faces. Our daughter caught the power of God's presence in that moment, and she couldn't hide her sadness any longer. Tears streamed down her cheeks. "Why is she crying?" people must have wondered.

In contrast, our five-year-old daughter seemed neutral about saying good-bye to our congregation. She was too young to bond with the church or to count up the cost of her parents' decisions.

In any given pastoral family, there may be several opinions about what losing a congregation means, just as there were in our family. Pastors usually receive top billing in the leaving news. "Alas, we are losing our pastor." Or "Thank God our pastor is finally leaving." But a pastor's family members may have practiced various other ministries that are also ending. The whole family must let go of tasks and relationships.

Leaving affords us the opportunity to view our family as a team. Seeing ourselves as a part of something bigger can be both excruciating and liberating. Excruciating, because working together requires conflict management and talking about hard issues. Liberating, because we won't feel so alone and we will discover the potential power of teamwork.

Creating a good good-bye for our family opens up the subject that has undoubtedly arisen more than once in our ministry, blending our family time and our work time. So old resentments begin to entangle themselves with new discernments. For all the positive aspects of the congregation, it can easily create divisions between pastors and their families. Pastors are torn. When things are going well at church, we worry about what we are ignoring at home, and vice versa. This could happen with any job, but the congregation is a shared job, and being a pastor is both a job and a role. The temple even came between the boy Jesus and his parents, didn't it?

We never perfectly balance our roles as pastor, spouse, and parent. That might happen in the next life, but in this life we muddle through. We get a sore neck looking at the tennis match in which one side is home and the other is church.

How do families work out the conflicts that arise when we make church another member of the family? With untold compromise and common goals. With exasperation, humor, and tenaciousness.

Martha and Mary got caught in the snare of trying to share ministry. Rather than recognize each other's unique style of ministry, each of them simply thought she had all that was needed to serve God. Finally, they met at the only place they could come together—in Jesus's presence.

Even when we feel hopelessly estranged or irreparably separated, we can meet at our common belief in a loving, forgiving God. By reaffirming what we have in common, we do not merely have to assume we are on separate pages.

In fact, we absolutely need one another to find what Jesus promised. Peace building requires more than one party. Peace talks won't happen if only one side shows up at the table. So we all have to show up at the kitchen table. Better make sure we have plenty of chairs. Our sense of call and duty will be there along with us. And our egos! Sometimes our egos require the most space.

Leaving uncovers old wounds, yet reaffirms life-giving strategies that worked for our families as we balanced congregation and home life. No matter how many sermons we preached and confirmation classes we taught about love and forgiveness, those principles will confound and humble us in the realities of home.

Here are some ideas about how to make a good good-bye for our families. This list is meant to generate your own list.

You know your unique family situation and what has worked in the past. Whatever works, do more of it!

1. *Simply pay attention.* Whereas the congregation is a constant beehive of people and activity, home can feel quite isolated. Families can get trapped in isolated spaces and problems. Ideally, a counselor or trusted mentor can help us avoid getting stuck in the old traps of isolation and stubborn positions. An outsider can help us feel less alone and can hear everyone out. Would it have helped our family to sit down with an outside pastor to talk about leaving? Undoubtedly. I was trying to be our daughter's mom and pastor simultaneously. That never worked. Even if we don't have an outside person to help us, we can respect one another with this technique. Set a timer for ten minutes, and let one person talk without anyone else interrupting. Give each family member a chance for his or her ten minutes of air time. Ten minutes proves to be enough time to say a few things and for others to settle down enough to listen. The ten-minute technique gives us a chance to respectfully listen to one another, or at least grudgingly.

2. *Draw some boundaries of care.* A good good-bye for our families means taking care to do no harm. When Kelly and Pastor Tom left their congregation to serve another one, they struggled with their differing feelings about the move. Tom wanted to go; Kelly wanted to stay. Knowing that every day could be a battleground of resentment and animosity, they consciously said that they would cut each other a lot of slack in the interim.

3. *Build your family team outside the congregation.* Family members need a space where they can live out a private life, not just a public ministry. Even if Advent is breathing down your neck, make a plan with your family to spend half a day together. The less complicated and expensive, the better. When was the last time you just played a game or took a walk together? Don't make this an intense event; just take some time to have fun. The teamwork will grow with trust. When pastors block out time to be with families, we model this value to our congregations.

4. *Take a balanced approach.* Have a conversation at home about the gifts and detriments of being a pastor's family. Illustrate each point by using something that weighs more or less.

5. *Remember the priesthood of all believers.* We know in theory that hope lies in stepping back from the business of the congregation and refocusing on the tenets of our faith—love and forgiveness. Forgiveness arises as the single most important skill we can learn and practice. But—ouch! ouch! Forgiveness can be so painful. How can we forgive others who see things so differently than we do? Now there's a question to bring to prayer and to the kitchen table. A question that will ultimately bring us back to a holy place, our faith.

For Reflection . . .

1. Who are your spouse's and children's closest church friends?

2. How has your family been part of the decision and process of saying good-bye?

3. What happens in your family when spouses disagree about major decisions?
4. What models of good good-byes have you noticed in other pastors' families?

Exit Marks the Spot

Before we cross that threshold on our final trip out the door, here are a few *ex*es for us to ponder.

Exit

For months or years, we walked in and out of the door at church. Off we strode (or slogged) each workday—to home calls, community meetings, hospital visits, and outdoor work parties—barely noticing the threshold over which we crossed.

But the last time is different. This time our destination *is* the door, not a hospital, home, or synod office beyond the door. During the weeks leading up to this moment, we inched closer and closer to the door. The square on our calendar marking our departure date even looked like an exit door. Preparations, conversations, and feelings all brought us nearer and nearer to this place. And now we're here—at the exit door and the exit interview.

Both in the secular world and in the religious world, an exit interview provides a learning opportunity for both the one leaving and those staying. As we get together, we can talk about what worked and what didn't work. Discussing lingering issues goes a long way toward tying up loose ends that we don't have to wonder about later. An exit interview with the congregation allows us the opportunity to look back on the ministry. We can do so in a reflective way by using an ancient Ignatian practice of evaluation called the Examen. In an Examen prayer, we *examine* the most life-giving and least life-giving sides of an experience, such as a pastorate. In an Examen prayer, we give thanks for the ways that God works through both life-giving and life-sapping experiences.

About five hundred years ago St. Ignatius wrote a book about the things that helped him in his prayer life. In his book he described a way to pray—the Examen. Ignatius understood that often it's hard to discern God's guidance in our lives. But Ignatius realized that, over time, when he prayed to God about his most life-giving moments (his consolations) and about his least life-giving times (his desolations), he began to see God's will for him much more clearly.

The beauty of practicing the Examen in an exit interview is that it is basic enough that we can pray it quite simply, yet profound enough that it enables us to uncover God's wisdom in our life together.

Before you meet for your exit interview, give participants a sheet on which to prepare reflections about the ministry's (1) most life-giving moments and (2) least life-giving times. At the exit interview, take time to listen and honor one another's reflections about your shared congregational experience.

Expirare

E*x* means "out" in Latin. As we say good-bye, we struggle to sort out the *ex* of *exire* (to go out) from the *ex* in *expirare* ("to go away"—from death). We die a little, or a lot, with each good-bye, and we get a glimpse of the big good-bye to come, the exit door through which every human being has exited this world. We are dying in some sense as we leave a congregation—even if a fantastic new call awaits us, even if we counted down the days to this moment (over several years!). We are dying to a particular experience with a one-of-a-kind community in which we practiced a unique role. We can't relive this experience anymore than we can relive a day on the calendar.

When we step out, we will of course carry the congregation with us. God's Holy Spirit never expires. God's realm will never be limited by buildings, no matter how magnificently holy or well-crafted the houses of God may be. We carry the people we love with us. And the ones with whom we tangled? We will carry them even longer and farther.

Child psychologist Jean Piaget defined the concept of *object permanence*, a developmental task that most babies master by their first birthday. Babies come to understand that even if they can't see, hear, or touch an object, the object still exists, which is a pretty important understanding when Mom or Dad says goodnight and goes to sleep in another room! Babies learn to trust that their loved one hasn't evaporated, and they don't need to cry all night.

Our developmental task as pastors saying good-bye is to relearn object permanence. The people with whom we worked, worshiped, and served continue to exist on the other side of the door through which we step out, even if we can't see, hear, or touch those beloved folks. We once clasped their hands as we shared Christ's peace. We once heard the confessions they whispered in our ear. We once splashed water on their hairless scalp. And now? We all continue to exist—in the object permanence of the universe and in the Holy Spirit. But we cannot necessarily reach through a door to touch one another any longer. Only Jesus could return through the barriers of death and a door to soothe his mourning band of followers.

Our most loving pastoral instincts, and our most stubborn natures, keep us from accepting object permanence. We insist that we simply must remain in the presence of our community. We worry that our community of Christ won't trust that we loved them or loved leading them, if we fail to appear. But they will.

X MARKS THE POINT OF NO RETURN

Our daughter's driver's ed teacher taught their class an important lesson about intersections and the X's therein. Once you drive over the middle of the X in an intersection, you have to keep going, even if the light turns yellow and then red. Her teacher called this moment of decision-making *the point of no return*. We also move into an intersection when we say goodbye to a congregation. Respecting the point of no return in the congregation I served and not turning back allowed me to follow through on my commitment to grieve my congregation and move on.

From the time I announced to the senior pastor that I was leaving, his words rang clearly in my head. "When you leave, you leave the congregation as well." Many people asked me about the practice of pastors moving on from both their jobs and their churches, and they expressed their dismay about this tradition. But I didn't challenge the tradition of leaving completely, simultaneously vacating both my office and my envelope number, even if doing so felt a little stark to me at the time.

Much later, after grieving the loss, I felt extremely thankful for the finality of walking out that church door and not turning back. Grieving would have been so much messier if I tried to morph into being a congregation member. Staying away forced me to accept things I never could have learned otherwise. The two-good-byes-in-one deal called me to a new congregation, even if that took time and tears. Leaving both role and home church enabled me to better understand and respect the unique role a pastor holds in the eyes of a congregation.

If a pastor is simply moving to serve another congregation, the question of whether that person can remain a member of the congregation is a moot point. But if you're retiring or reinventing yourself in a new vocation, I can attest to the benefit of feeling sad but staying away. Grief brings growth.

Two members of the church council conducted my exit interview the day after my final sermon and party. I answered their perfunctory questions, but it was nerve-wracking to sit at that round table in the church library with the exit door in view. I was spent from the good-byes and eager to start the daring journey. They asked me about my church plans, hedging around the question of my finding a new church home. "When I walk out that door (I pointed), I will be walking out for good."

And so I did. The exit bar squeaked when I pushed down on it, as always. My foot stepped on the metal threshold one more time. Feel it. This is good-bye.

For Reflection . . .

1. What do you hope for in your exit interview? Write
   out your own agenda and expectations to share with
   the planners before your exit interview.
2. Do you agree with your denomination's policy about
   congregation membership after departure? If so, how
   do you think the policy will ease your way? If not,
   how will you express your disagreement?
3. What prayer will you carry in your pocket as you
   walk over the threshold a final time?

Our Last, Last Supper

Jesus wrote the book on good-bye . . . and we get to read
it. Before Jesus said good-bye to his friends to enter a new
world, he shared a last supper with his disciples. How do we
finalize a time of shared ministry? According to Jesus, we do
so by getting together to celebrate and confirm the nature
of that ministry—by sharing a meal, seasoned with meaning,
prayer, and holy rites. Jesus showed us how to combine good-
bye with a meal.

We pastors should be adept at marking good-byes, because
we regularly shared with a congregation Jesus's good-bye
meal, communion. We practiced Jesus's model of saying good-
bye without even realizing that we were doing so. We offered
words of love to put in our pocket, a swallow of sweetness to
ease our way.

The Last Supper can serve as a symbol of our pastoral
tenure in a congregation, all the years we shared with this faith
community wrapped into one meal with Jesus. According

to our clocks and calendars, our time together as a church may have measured five years or twenty years. But in God's *kairos* time, our common endeavor may have looked like one continuous meal in which we were fed by Jesus and empowered for community service.

JESUS FED HIS DISCIPLES DURING THEIR THREE YEARS TOGETHER

Ever since that first day when he provided his disciples a clear purpose with a call to follow him, Jesus nurtured his disciples with forgiveness, prayer, and adventure. And at the Last Supper, Jesus fed his disciples one more time.

We have fed parishioners multiple holy suppers, often matter-of-factly, like a mom who puts forth a meal on the table day after day. No fanfare, just faithfulness. And God has fed us over our entire ministry as well, even during those meals when we ran out of wine or dropped crumbs of too-stale bread all over the floor.

God has shown up every Sunday, giving us enough spiritual food to write another sermon, lead another staff meeting, begin another stewardship campaign, search for another youth director. God has fed us with communion and reminded us of something we might not have noticed—that this meal keeps us going, and this meal helps us say good-bye.

JESUS GAVE THEM SOMETHING TO REMEMBER

When they shared their last meal, Jesus knew his time with his disciples was running out. Preparing to part with special friends, Jesus pleaded, "Don't forget me, okay?" More importantly, "Don't forget my love for you, and your love for others." Jesus used bread and wine, elements that his disciples could taste and swallow, as a means to help them remember. Forgetting Jesus would mean forgetting the center of their lives. So Jesus tried to help out his disciples (and us) with an opportunity for experiential learning: "In case your mind forgets me, I'll give your body some reminders." The softness of just-washed feet. The oaky undertones of a vintage red, an aftertaste of the feast to come. And what do we carry away within us to remember a particular ministry? Maybe we can dig up a little soil from beside the front door and take it home to plant a seed for the future. Or we could ask the quilters to make us a blanket of brightness and warmth. Finally, we can take along the mutual conversation and consolation of the saints as another reminder of important discussions and meaningful work done side by side.

JESUS GATHERED THE BODY OF CHRIST

At the Last Supper, Jesus's friends climbed the stairs to a specially designated spot for their good-bye meal. The disciples' feet bore the history of the ground they'd covered to get to the upper room. This intimate group had walked with Jesus over three years. When Jesus washed their feet, he must have felt the blisters and calluses of ministry. Jesus's twelve friends—a communion of saints whom Jesus chose—were the ones who walked the miles, witnessed Jesus's words, got wet in a boat, tore the bread into pieces for all, and wondered and wondered and wondered. In washing their feet and calling them to serve one another just as he served them, Jesus once again gave them one another, "the body of Christ."

The body of Christ arrives in more than one form—as a piece of bread and in the way our upper arms touch the upper arms of other members of the body of Christ who surround us at the table. A pastor hands out a piece of bread and utters Jesus's words, "The body of Christ, given for you," a plural you! Each of us at the table is part of the church, the body of Christ that sustains and challenges those in its ranks. We discover Christ in front of us and surrounding us at this farewell meal.

At communion we come together, never knowing for sure who might be at the table when this body of Christ gathers again. For all the things in our control on Sunday mornings—which pew to sit in, whom to talk to, how much to put in the offering plate—communion always holds a surprise. We're never 100 percent sure where each of us will end up each Sunday at the communion table, but we trust that each time we receive bread and wine, we also receive the body of Christ—a community of faith and farewell—on each side of us.

At Supper, Jesus Prayed His Good-bye

Jesus didn't just talk to his disciples at the Last Supper; Jesus talked to God about his disciples, the ones whom Jesus loved. And what a model he gives us as we move into good-bye. Many necessary tasks and potential minefields lie ahead on our departure journey. The shift out of a parish involves packing up, commemorating our shared endeavor, and working day after day to maintain respect, boundaries, and courage.

Jesus offered us a model to ground and lead us through the hectic days ahead. Before that last crumb of bread is swept up, before the last sandal slaps down the stairs, before the drips of wine soak into the table linens—while we are still together—we can talk to God about the ones we love.

We can begin our good-bye with prayer, or rather, continue our ministry of prayer. Of course we have called out to God about the young and old with whom we served, about the bonds and grudges accumulated along the way. Now we are again invited to talk to God about the least of these and the most of these, the one and the everyone.

Jesus Taught His Disciples a Daring Truth

"Who will separate us from the love of Christ?" we read in Romans 8:35. Neither life nor death, nor our collar nor an altar rail, nothing can separate us, and yet we anticipate the time when we are no longer together as a community. As we prepare to say good-bye, even the communion rail may seem like a line marking our separation—the ones who will stay, the one who will go. But God always steps across any line we draw between others and ourselves. No one is left alone.

Jesus taught his disciples this daring truth: "I will not leave you orphaned; I am coming to you. In a little while the world will no longer see me, but you will see me; because I live, you also will live" (John 14:18). We can dare to leave one another and follow God to new places, because we will never be completely separated. Jesus could look his disciples in the eye to say good-bye because of this new promise. God's Holy Spirit will always connect us.

Pastors continue to share the mystery of Jesus's parting gift of presence with God's people every time we pass out the bread. Jesus left, Jesus is still here; Jesus left, Jesus is still here. Tear off a bite of the spiritual life. We feel alone, we are together in Christ; we feel alone, we are together in Christ.

JESUS, REMEMBER ME

This is where we began our ministry, at the altar, called to a community of Word and Sacrament. This is where we can begin to say good-bye, because communion means more than good-bye. Communion symbolizes "See you again someday," when we join together at God's table.

How many times did Jesus say good-bye to his disciples on the night of that first Last Supper? Did the group linger at the table, hover at the door, and share one last conversation out on the driveway? That's how we often say good-bye, reluctant to part from our loved ones. And at the last minute, to delay the moment of separation and extend the love, we feed them one more time. We pull out the leftovers we have packed up for them—turkey sandwiches, a little something for the way home.

That's what God gives us as we leave the table for good and leave for separate places—pastors east and parishioners west—a little something for the way. Taste and see.

We will share Jesus's story and his way of doing life, no matter where our clean feet take us next.

For Reflection . . .

1. Take time each day to talk to God about the ones you love.
2. How have you remembered Jesus during this exit period? How has Jesus remembered you?

3. What did this congregation teach you about God's surprises?

Farewell

Like any good mystery, the Mystery of Faith begins with a death. Christ has died. Christ is risen. Christ will come again. Leaving a congregation where you have served as a pastor begins with a death, too. For whatever reason, the time has come to bury a particular experience, to grieve it enough to move on. Like any death, the process of leaving and separation hurts. The pain is acute enough to make you notice it. Like any death, an air of mystery can't be shaken. It can be hard to find words to explain the end to yourself and others.

Like any death, this one calls for a funeral—a funeral for an era, not a person. By honoring an era of ministry and relationships, a community finishes its business.

How do pastors and congregants conduct funerals for the one(s) they have lost—for the pastor who is leaving and for the congregation being left behind? We can commemorate the ending of a pastorate by using what we have learned about death and life from all the funerals we have led over the years.

We Need Funerals so that We Can Celebrate and Mourn Together

A funeral is a public rite that honors a life. Funerals don't distinguish between a person who was one day old and a person who was one hundred years old when he or she died.

Each person deserves a ritual acknowledging that his or her
life belongs to God. Each community needs an opportunity
to say good-bye and to witness the mystery of life and death.

Communities need a chance to gather to give thanks
for a life that touched our lives and to hear God's promises
proclaimed in scriptures about eternal life. We long to sing
our dear departed's favorite hymns. We depend on funerals
to serve as nets that will capture stories about the essence of
a person's life. The funeral liturgy speaks to God's presence
with the grieving as well as God's special care for the one
who died.

We Need to Proclaim Our Belief in Life after Death

When Jesus rose from the dead on Easter, all good-byes were
reframed in hope. Congregations are not going to witness
their former pastors rising from the dead (even if they show
up each Sunday in the back pew). Pastorates definitely end,
as painful as that might feel. But Jesus's resurrection assures
us the spirit of the church community lives on. A good-bye
service confirms both of these truths.

We Need the Healing Funerals Offer

People don't usually spend a lot of time at funerals going on
about what a blankety-blank the departee was. A dead person's
flaws may be an undercurrent at his or her funeral, but funerals
are typically about remembering the best in a person, even if
the best is a tiny germ. The funeral of a pastorate may enable
a congregation to conduct this same exercise of looking for
the best, perhaps in the very place where hope had been lost.

We can use all these death-and-life lessons to create a good-bye service that includes both the reality of separation and the hope of something more. Search the Internet for possibilities or ask staff of your judicatory for suggestions, such as "A Service for Ending a Pastoral Relationship" in the book *Beginning Ministry Together: The Alban Handbook for Clergy Transitions*.[2]

Our pastoral farewell services may touch on many theological themes, such as joy, incarnation, trust, and continuity. As we gather for one more worship service, the upper octaves of the organ celebrate the life, music, and story we shared. The deepest tones of the organ bellow out the subtext of the service: After today, our pastor will no longer be in that chancel in front of us. We love a leader who loves us. A pastor's departure may feel a bit like God's incarnated love is heading out the door. Don't go, God!

On the other side of this farewell service, a new, unknown era awaits. A congregation asks itself, "Who will we be without this person who cared for us, who enlivened our church, who worried about the operations and details, who planned the liturgies that fed us, who faithfully showed up, who loved our children?"

At our farewell service, our recessional leads to a processional, a line of God's servants working throughout time. We call it the cloud of witnesses. When we step out of a church building, we are stepping into God's larger sanctuary. We join a line of prophets, saints, and small-town pastors who found out that God's love endures beyond farewell.

For Reflection . . .

1. How are saying hello to a congregation and saying good-bye to a congregation related?
2. What key ingredients must be part of your good-bye?
3. What does your farewell service reveal to you about the power of liturgy?
4. Write the prayers for your service.

PART 2

The Long Good-bye

Losing My Place

I just glanced up to see your face
As you received God's words of grace
I just glanced up to see your face
and suddenly I lost my place
I looked back down, scanned Holy text
Had not a clue which word came next
The silence stretched, the tension grew
Where was my place? What should I do?
I split the difference, picked a word
Continued on, God's message heard
I just glanced up to see your face
And suddenly I lost my place
How years dissolve 'til ends astound
Some places cannot be refound

Why Does "So Long" Take So Long?

I used to tell couples before I performed their marriage cere-
mony that I would be marrying them for the first time, but
they would actually get married several times. They would

marry again the day they adopted a baby or the day one of them lost a job or the day they said good-bye to a parent. Marriage happens again and again; so does good-bye. We might imagine that we are saying good-bye on the day of our last worship service or at the moment we walk out the door. And it's true that we say an official, even sacramental good-bye at those times. But we will say good-bye again on the first Sunday we are not at church and on the first Christmas Eve that happens without us and on the day we see a former parishioner in the grocery store and her hug reaches a hole in our heart.

But we don't expect our good-byes to take this long! After all, as pastors in charge of congregations, we have set the schedules and managed events. Lenten services on Wednesday nights. Congregational meeting on the last Sunday of January. Blessing of the backpacks in September. Ever since we left, however, we can't seem to get the end of grief to stick on our calendar.

Why does "so long" take so long? Every grief can linger and dredge up past griefs, but leaving a pastoral call is a particular grief. We lose our congregation as well as our job. We lose a place that we call God's house. I missed *my place*. I rode my bike up the hill to my former church predawn so that I could touch the door and somehow connect to my former life. I even "stalked" my congregation on its website. I clicked on the virtual tour, and there I was—back in the library, at home in the sacristy once again.

"So long" can take so long because the particular grief of leaving a parish includes both the outward grief of leaving people behind and the inward grief of leaving an identity behind. "So long" takes so long because transitioning from

"God's house" to our home, and not being immersed in church life every day, can feel like culture shock.

Finally, "so long" takes so long for the same reason that sermons often take so long. When we preach the Sunday text, we must stay on one page of Scripture and preach about one assigned story. We can't just escape to our favorite or less complex passages. So it takes awhile to research and ponder what we will say. Leaving takes awhile, too. It happens fragile page by fragile page, but gradually enough pages accumulate to reveal the gold on the edges.

Culture Shock

When I was twenty-three years old, I signed up for culture shock. I had just finished college and took a job teaching school in a rural area, an environment that felt very unfamiliar to my youthful spirit. As I sat in the teachers' lounge each day, the middle-aged teachers talked excitedly about things like their new washing machines and dryers. Their settled lives, so different from the adventurous life of a college student that I'd just left behind, looked like jail to me in my early twenties. "I've got to get out of here!" I promised myself. And soon I did get out. I moved on to an even more intense experience of culture shock: I joined the Peace Corps and moved to Kingston, Jamaica.

My Peace Corps experience in Kingston was ushered in by my home stay in a dank house occupied by an embittered older woman. During my twelve weeks of orientation, dark aqua walls pressed in on me in my new bedroom. Plastic streamers hung in the doorways to keep flies from moving through the house. Gray boiled bananas, yellow *chocho* (a prickly skinned, pear-shaped legume), and a tasty but tiny piece of chicken greeted me at the dinner table each evening. Those washers and dryers I'd heard about back in the teachers' lounge seemed much more appealing now, as I scrubbed my laundry by hand in a plastic tub behind the house.

On the first morning that I walked from my host's home to the Peace Corps office, a dog ran out from the neighbor's yard and bit me on the ankle. Welcome to Jamaica! I wiped away the tears, and the Peace Corps nurse wiped away the blood. Still, as a resilient twenty-three-year-old, I tenaciously continued to adjust to my new surroundings. Every morning, I walked past the prolific trash, the chiding children, the loose dogs, the honking traffic, the broken glass, the holes in the sidewalk, and the mentally ill man who always walked around the neighborhood naked.

Thank God for Peace Corps friends! We bonded over finding scorpions in our shoes and dealing with Jamaica's cultural surprises during those initial weeks of training. Here's how we survived culture shock: We learned to love Jamaica for its people, quirks, reggae, and stunning beauty. We hopped buses to the market, mountains, and beaches. We amassed our sense of adventure, curiosity, and humor so that we could learn together, rather than look back alone. We found a church.

Leaving parish ministry also lands pastors smack dab in culture shock, stretched between the knowns of a role and community and the unknowns of change. We tear the fabric of the known, and the unknown can't merely be stitched on to the raveled edge. "What have I done?" we may wonder.

Culture shock requires us to undertake large tasks: letting go and enduring a time of wondering where we fit in a new world. Managing culture shock is about not merely letting go of an old life but trying to find some footholds or handholds for a new life. But culture shock also holds an air of excitement and stimulation. When we climb out of old ruts, we discover new worlds, new ways, and new perspectives about God. Letting go of the old structures can actually be liberating, as long as we are willing to learn a new normal and trust that we're not alone in our learning.

For Reflection . . .

1. Culture shock represents a time of suspense. We honestly wonder if we will ever be able to make the transition from one world to another. Plot the story arc of your journey of leaving. What precipitated the change? What were the points of tension along the way? Are you still in suspense?

2. Culture shock is a time of going back and forth between the familiar past and the radically new present. To what from the past and present do you cling most fiercely? What changes do you resist? What changes do you anticipate?

Alone

When we are no longer insulated from loneliness, sin, and emptiness by scores of people, grief and culture shock may slam into us. Suddenly we have only ourselves for company. We are alone.

Those first days home (after we've finally slept enough to feel physically rested) can be unsettling. We have untied the

ties that bind, and now we have only loose ends to show for
our efforts. We went from full calendars to temporarily empty
calendars. We moved from knowing where we were going to
not being sure what's next. After taking care of others for so
long, at this juncture we need to take care of ourselves. After
all, we left a place, a job, and a community all at once. So it
shouldn't be surprising when we find ourselves exhibiting
many of the grief stages we've watched others face over the
years—like sadness, anger, and ennui.

I didn't really realize how alone I felt until one morning
when I went to visit a pastor friend at her congregation.
She was sitting with several older people in the fellowship
hall—laughing and joking around. The contrast between my
silent house and that lively gathering seemed pointedly stark.
I wanted to stay. And, although I didn't know it at the time, I
felt envious of my friend and her continuing role as pastor. She
belonged to those people. She could still work at God's house
and share laughs and holy moments with her congregation.

To escape my loneliness, I often walked around a local
lake. I walked with friends from outside of the congregation
who listened to me talk about those first days of confusion
and sadness. I walked by myself, praying for help.

As my literal and figurative steps of departure accumulated around that lake, I noticed that I didn't know most of
the people I passed, a discovery that deepened my sense of
aloneness. In a church, we get the false illusion that we know
the whole world, because we do know the whole world
of a congregation. But in a larger environment, we quickly
discover that we are surrounded by strangers—strangers who
seem perfectly fulfilled, even though they may have no idea
what Setting 2 of the liturgy sounds like. When I left parish
ministry, I met several practicing Buddhists and marveled at

how different their worldview was from mine. I didn't realize that I had been judging or sorting people based on their membership in the church, but I found it hard to relate to a world that didn't know or care about the church. Was God really so much bigger than I imagined?

Even encounters with people from my former life could reiterate my sense of disconnection. While walking around the lake one morning, I ran into an elderly couple who belonged to the congregation I had served. I was so astonished to see them. Somehow I wasn't sure that all those congregation members still existed in this world! They gave me a huge hug, and said, "We still miss you." I had no idea how thirsty I was for their words until I heard them say, "Pastor Mary." They still loved me, remembered me, felt connected to me. Jesus talks about living water. That couple surely dipped a refreshing cup of kindness for me that morning. But as we continued on, each going in a different direction, I was reminded I was not their pastor. I was not anyone's pastor.

And I wouldn't be anyone's pastor during special church seasons either. On that first Christmas Eve after I left my call as children's pastor, the hour of the traditional family service rolled round and unnerved me with grief. I suddenly realized that I wasn't at church for *my* service. I used to be the one who sat near the youth, ready to help them if they lost their place while narrating the service. I used to be there when their adolescent cockiness faded and the holiness of the night and weight of their leadership roles crept in. I dearly missed being a partner with God's people and my best self for God during that moment.

The aloneness we feel after we leave reveals our sense of separation not only from beloved people but also from a purpose that transcended our own lives. The congregation gave us a place to rise above ourselves. We *had* to show up and pray at that hospital bed. We were *expected* to be there every week for the Wednesday night program. Those expectations provided us with structure and purpose. Ministry toned our soul, like swimming laps in baptismal waters. Even if the work sometimes required hurdling tall inner resistance, we were bound and privileged by God's call to show up for others. We got over ourselves because, as pastors, we had to.

But what if we can't get over ourselves when no one is demanding that we focus beyond ourselves, when no one calls us beyond our baser instincts—when we're alone? What if we can't hide behind the busyness of our role or assume that God's call to deeply care for another will come knocking on our door? What if the human condition sneaks up on us in a new world? What if, with the apostle Paul, we worry about the good we want to do—and that the pastoral role helped us to do—versus the self-absorbed pettiness and narrowness into which we so easily fall?

The reason we could show up for others is that God showed up for us. And leaving, with grief and loss, certainly doesn't change God's availability. Good-bye just leaves God hoping we will notice that we're not alone, even when we are.

For Reflection . . .

1. Write a poem about your aloneness. Haiku, limerick, sonnet—any form will do.
2. How do you feel about no longer being surrounded by so many parishioners?
3. In what surprising places beyond the congregation have you discovered God at work?

Church Time

World travelers find out that we become most vulnerable to the pain of culture shock when we're moving from one time zone to another. As we suddenly find ourselves in a strange new world, our stamina may diminish and our minds can struggle to process all the change. Over the years, church time slowly but surely shaped our internal pastoral clocks. As we leave, we step out of church time into other time zones.

Church time ensured that we never marked time the way the rest of the world did. We rarely shouted "TGIF!" because Friday was just the beginning of another part of our work-week. On the rare Saturdays when we weren't preaching the next day, we carried around a nagging suspicion all day that we were forgetting something. And keeping the Sabbath? We never knew exactly how to make that happen. We worked on everyone else's Sabbath. We barely needed an alarm clock on Sundays, so attuned were our bodies to the centrality of weekly worship.

Ironically, part of the predictability of church time rested in its unpredictability. We always needed to be ready, or at least willing, to drop the work we expected to be doing and pick up the crises that suddenly presented themselves. Many days we felt as if we'd accomplished none of the goals for which we had planned. The bulletin, newsletter, and phone messages simply piled up when a member's sudden death or hospitalization pulled us away from our desks.

Church time made us live the rhythms of days, weeks, and months in a parish-driven way. We kept a mental calendar in our heads and could name the dates of the Sundays a couple of months out. Even the yearly calendar took on a particular shape based on church time. The Friday after Thanksgiving was not just Black Friday; it was the Friday before Advent 1. Martin Luther King Jr. Day was not just a day off; it marked two days or two weeks before Ash Wednesday. Annual events such as Stewardship Sunday and the congregational meeting influenced the way we organized our lives as much as the solstice, the equinox, and Super Bowl Sunday. Just as people living in a four-season climate periodically trot out their winter jackets or summer shorts, we unshelved our favorite Christmas books and six months later fetched our green stoles.

Church time also gave us a sense of the church's "fiscal" year, which always commenced on Advent 1 with prophecies about Jesus's birth and continued on through Christmas and Epiphany, Lenten disciplines, and Easter season Sundays. Before long we counted—Pentecost 24, Pentecost 25, Pentecost 26—and then we started back at Advent 1 anew. Year after year we longed for Jesus in Advent, contemplated the cross during Lent, and walked with Jesus during the multiple Sundays of Pentecost. But even as the church year unfolded again and again, even as we retold the old, old story, we never ceased to be surprised. Even though we celebrated the same holy days every year, we never remembered exactly how Good Friday felt until we stood before the congregation to read Jesus's words from the cross. We never quite recalled the excitement of Pentecost until the red banners hung all around us.

The story was always the same, a tale of life, death, and resurrection. But each year the texts spoke a little differently. And this year, the year of our leaving, our life is the text. In our stories of good-bye and hello, God reveals a time even more sacred than church time. Now is *kairos* time, a sense of time that is simply God's to define. In the fullness of *kairos* time—no matter what the clock or church calendar might say—God says, "It's time!" Time to turn our shoes around, time to worship in new pews, time to turn the page.

For Reflection . . .

1. How might you view and structure your days and years when you're not a pastor?
2. Complete this stem with your own examples: You will know you've let go of church time when . . .

    You forget what time choir rehearsal started.

    You imagine that you could go to a play or concert on Saturday night.

    You figure out which television shows air on Wednesday evening.

    You can look at a purple-hewed sunset without wondering whether Easter will be early or late next year.

Set Apart, Set Aside

Do we stop being pastors when we stop working as pastors? That question nagged at Ron as he tried to figure out whether he was grieving the loss of his relationship with one particular congregation or the broader loss of a role and identity. Ron's question became especially difficult to answer when others asked him, "Are you still in the ministry?"

During his pastorate, Ron had taught that in God's priesthood of all believers, everyone is called to various aspects of God's ministry in the home, in the wider community, in the congregation, and—for some—in paid employment. But he realized that unlike pastoral ministry, most professions don't involve the expectation that people hear and answer a call as a prerequisite to doing the work. In most professions, people are hired to do a job. In the church, though, pastors are understood to be called first by God and then by a particular community. From day one pastors are *ordained*, set apart for a specific role in the faith community. Leaving what has been ordained can feel complicated.

Frankly, after going on disability, Ron worried much more about being set aside than being set apart. He sat in the pew on Ash Wednesday, and for the first time since his good-bye to parish ministry, he was not marking ashen crosses on people's foreheads. Ron had briefly considered boycotting the worship service, not sure he wanted to face the fact that he was no longer the leader and afraid that he might feel too sad. But he soon gave up the notion of a one-man protest. Ron showed up. The congregation provided much-needed community. He knew that his need to be with God's people was stronger than his feelings of grief. Leaders come and go; communities continue. And so Ron sat in the pew, thinking, wondering, feeling a bit lost, and trying to be hopeful. He felt wistful when he saw his pastor up at the altar, and when he stood and walked down the aisle to receive a sooty reminder, he moved more slowly than usual.

Ron had surrendered to going on disability because he struggled more and more with back pain. Ironically, on this night denoting the start of Lent, a long-ago memory returned to Ron and made him chuckle. Ron remembered way back to his first Ash Wednesday as a pastor, when he didn't realize that you had to add some oil to the ashes to make them stick together and adhere to a person's forehead. The first parishioner stepped up to Ron, and Ron dipped his thumb in the small dish of ashes he had prepared on Shrove Tuesday. He tried to smudge a cross on the parishioner's forehead, but the ashes fell apart and trickled down her nose and cheeks. The same thing happened to everyone in the line. In fact, no one actually walked out of church that night with a cross on his or her forehead!

At the beginning of his ordained ministry, Ron learned that it takes both elements, ash and oil, to make a cross. The ash grounds us in the soil from which we were created and where we will someday join the ranks of our buried or strewn ancestors. The oil ties us to the anointing of biblical leaders and the baptisms of innumerable children of God.

This Ash Wednesday evening, at the end of his ordained ministry, Ron touched the cross on his forehead. He wasn't sure if the major piece that slipped out from under him was a disc or his pastoral identity. *Was* he still a pastor? Yes. In the cross are held together ash and oil, past and present, our hopes and fears, our images of ourselves and God's vision for us. They could not fall apart.

For Reflection . . .

1. Do you introduce yourself as a pastor when you're not working as a pastor?
2. When did you know you were called to be a pastor?
3. How would you feel if no one ever called you "pastor" again?

Mum's the Word: Ezekiel

Neither the books Pastor Ellen studied nor the consultant she hired nor the prayers she fervently offered had been able to quell the conflict that had arisen in the last congregation she served. Therefore, retiring early finally seemed like the best option. But even though she had said good-bye to a church, Ellen wasn't really ready to retire. She still had much to give a congregation, and she felt lost without her role and work. As she stumbled through her transitional days, she took refuge in the things that had always brought her joy and comfort— walks, concerts, and her grandchildren. She also found herself relishing experiences she hadn't taken time for while she was serving a parish. At the top of her mental to-do list: reading and reflecting on the Bible simply to hear what God might be saying rather than to prepare a sermon or Bible study.

Fearing that without work her bones might dry up, Ellen felt drawn to Ezekiel. She had always identified with him, for she considered herself a prophet in her own ministry. Her forte was to speak the truth about injustice and not be cowed by people who didn't want to hear that truth. So, she wandered among the chapters of Ezekiel, looking for life, and happened on a story that she didn't remember ever reading before.

> Then the hand of the LORD was upon me there; and he said to me, Rise up, go out into the valley, and there I will speak with you. So I rose up and went out into the valley; and the glory of the LORD stood there, like the glory that I had seen by the river Chebar; and I fell on my face. The spirit entered into me, and set me on my feet; and he spoke with

me and said to me: Go, shut yourself inside your house. As
for you, mortal, cords shall be placed on you, and you shall
be bound with them, so that you cannot go out among
the people; and I will make your tongue cling to the roof
of your mouth, so that you shall be speechless and unable
to reprove them; for they are a rebellious house. But when
I speak with you, I will open your mouth, and you shall
say to them, "Thus says the Lord GOD"; let those who will
hear, hear; and let those who refuse to hear, refuse; for they
are a rebellious house.

Ezekiel 3:22–27

Ellen felt nonplussed by Ezekiel's paradoxical message from
God. Immediately after being called by God, Ezekiel was
rendered speechless and restricted from going out among
the people. Ellen read and reread the story. The sequence of
events made as little sense to her as her premature retirement.
Why would God silence a prophet? Had God silenced her?

When she had stepped out of her pulpit that last time,
Ellen hadn't realized that she could be saying good-bye to her
prophetic call. But increasingly, that seemed to be the case.
After all, she wondered daily why her purpose in life seemed
to die before she did. She continued to hold strong views
about how the world should work, based on God's kingdom
vision. But there was no one to listen. Maybe she was no
longer called to speak? She wondered.

At least Ellen found a soul mate in Ezekiel. "Go, shut
yourself inside your house," God had instructed him. Ellen
understood that sense of being sequestered. Captured by
her sense of kinship with the prophet, she read more about
Ezekiel. Bible scholars, she learned, surmise that God silenced

him for seven years. Ellen contemplated the possible intent of God's messages to Ezekiel and his community. Was Ezekiel being humbled or empowered through his silence? Prophets had urged silent protests throughout the centuries to draw attention to injustices. Silence could be a powerful tool.

Now it struck her as ironic, though. In her pastoral ministry, Ellen cared fervently about giving a voice to the voiceless, and now she was the one who didn't have a pulpit or a congregation. "But prophets are not built for retirement," thought Ellen. The world still needed her, even if the church did not seem to want her. Ellen could listen, whether or not she had a place to speak. In her listening, she felt tied to Ezekiel. In her silence, she felt tied to the silenced ones of the world.

As a pastor, Ellen reflected, she had hoped and trusted that she was speaking for God. Now she would listen, and wait with Ezekiel and the voiceless, for God to speak in her.

For Reflection . . .

1. How would you characterize your ministry in the setting you have left or are leaving?
2. Do you have a next act up your sleeve? What might that be?
3. How could a period of silence, such as Ezekiel experienced, serve your ministry at this moment?
4. If you feel like you have lost your voice, write down the message you would like to offer to a willing listener.

Untying the Ties That Bind

Hymn writer John Fawcett (1740–1817) was ordained as a Baptist minister in rural England in 1765. After serving a small country church for seven years, he was invited to London to pastor a wealthier and more esteemed congregation. He accepted the call and preached his farewell sermon, the wagon with his possessions ready to roll out of town. But an outpouring of grief and love by his parishioners made him decide to stay instead. The experience led Fawcett to write his well-known hymn, "Blest Be the Tie that Binds."

Blest be the tie that binds
our hearts in Christian love;
the fellowship of kindred minds
is like to that above.

Before our Father's throne
we pour our ardent prayers;
our fears, our hopes, our aims are one,
our comforts and our cares.

We share each other's woes,
our mutual burdens bear;
and often for each other flows
the sympathizing tear.

When we asunder part,
it gives us inward pain;
but we shall still be joined in heart,
and hope to meet again.

In just a few short lines, Fawcett captured many of the sentiments we have explored in this book—namely, that pastors and parishioners share a special bond based on unity in Christ's word and mission. Fawcett's poignant words proved so true that they have endured for hundreds of years.

Like Fawcett, some pastors will unload the cart and stay, in spite of all the reasons they've considered leaving. But even if we delay a departure, we will inevitably face a good-bye someday, when we retire or receive a call to a new opportunity. And on that day, we can sing Fawcett's poignant words at our farewell service and know that the beauty and authenticity of the words were honed by his real-life grief.

After departing, however, we can take another clue from Fawcett's life—not "turn the wagon around," but "pour your love and loss into something creative." For Fawcett, that endeavor turned out to be a poem. He flung his net wide enough to capture the intense feelings swirling around him and gathered those emotions into a poem, a poem that became a hymn—four stanzas received from the Spirit and given back to God and the church Fawcett loved. He used his gift of writing to reach others.

As pastors, we regularly wrote as part of the job. Every Sunday, we faced a sermon deadline. We wrote prayers, newsletter blurbs, and blogs. We crafted Bible studies, monthly and annual reports, and stewardship invitation letters. I have recommended several writing ideas in this book, and if you like to write, you can emulate Fawcett or your favorite hymn writers or poets. But there are dozens of other outlets for expressing the feelings that arise when we leave a congregation. To arouse your own creativity, here are thirteen ideas—one for each of the bars in "Blest Be the Tie that Binds"—for ways to dedicate our emotions and spirits into tributes to the ones we left behind.

1. Tend a garden at home or in a community garden.
2. Practice the arts, such as woodworking, clock making, quilting, knitting.
3. Train for a long walk, bicycle trip, or backpacking journey.
4. Advocate for the needs of "the least of these."
5. Research your family history, and share your findings.
6. Continue your education through classes, elder hostels, and online learning.
7. Improve your cooking skills.
8. Tutor adults and children in schools or libraries.
9. Participate in a retreat from the Ignatian or another tradition.
10. Learn a new language and go volunteer in the place where they speak the language.
11. Mentor a new church leader.
12. Travel around the block or around the world.
13. Photograph or sketch the wonders that happen right outside your window.

You could undoubtedly come up with baker's dozens of your own ideas, but here's one more, for the letter writers among us. One pastor, after leaving his parish of twenty years, took a retreat at a friend's cabin. During his retreat days, he wrote letters to ten unforgettable members of his congregation. He knew he would never mail the letters, but he hoped the letters would help him release some of the emotions that churned around inside him, an important step in his letting go. Most of the letters were written to people with whom he felt strong connections, but having witnessed many congregational members face divorce during his pastorates, he knew that we can stay as intimately tied to people we dislike as to people we like. So several of the letters were written to "thorn in the flesh" people he wanted to let go of. As he composed the letters, no matter how he felt about each person, he searched for ways to say the things he really wanted to say. He tried not to analyze the relationships; he simply tried to express his truth. Then he shredded the letters.

This letter-writing exercise reflects what Fawcett's words demonstrated—that for all the issues and problems of the church as an institution, departure can reveal the core strength of the body of Christ—our shared faith. Our shared faith bound us when we could have fallen apart because of our differences. Our shared faith blessed our lives in incredible ways and witnessed to others. Our shared faith assures us now that "nothing can separate us from the love of Christ Jesus." The love of Christ is where we met, and we can trust that somehow our spirits will always be joined there.

For Reflection . . .

1. The congregational ties that bind us can unfortunately become the ties that blind us from the other essential ties in our life—like family ties and friendships. What relationships do you need to rebind, post pastorate?
2. How have you worked through change and grief in the past?
3. Which pastors have you admired for the way they said good-bye and moved on?

New Life

As Christians we believe that the road to new life passes through a neighborhood called Death to the Old Life. That sounds like a pretty rough trip, so we put off making the journey. Instead, we cling to our old, familiar lives with their well-worn habits, traditions, and pitfalls.

As pastors we sometimes hold on tenaciously to a known life in a church, even though we have a sense that we should move on. After all, we already know when to order the palms for Palm Sunday, the buses for Bible school, and the poinsettias for Christmas. And the new life of unfamiliar places and people frightens us—too many unknowns. In our heart, of course, we believe that new life *should* sound appealing; Christ is risen, indeed! But the mysteries and risks of change—like feeling unwelcome, misunderstood, or vulnerable—make us swallow our proclamation.

You would think clergy would be experts at embracing new life after talking about it in church so much. Each year, at the beginning of Lent, we turned toward the cross and said we wanted to follow Jesus to new life there. The promises of new life held water during Lent—living water in the well, healing water in the pool of Siloam, soothing water in the foot-washing basin. Even on those Good Fridays in the shadow of the cross, we cheered for new life. "Don't worry, Jesus," we whispered to him as he hanged on the cross. "We read ahead in the story . . . and we know the ending. You'll be alive again in no time!"

But Jesus knew a truth we can never quite hold on to for long, even after all those Lents and Holy Weeks: New life always arrives via small, medium, and large deaths. Small deaths, like saying good-bye to our habits and routines; medium deaths, like bidding farewell to our assumptions about safety and security; and large deaths, like realizing we will never be the same person in our new life that we were in our former life. Jesus drags us to resurrection via this route anyway. And as we make the journey, God dares us to simply stop looking—even for an hour or a day—at the things that we imagine are saving us and instead to notice something new.

When I think of dying to the past and opening myself to new life, I remember a silly little sound bite from an unlikely source. You probably keep quotes from Teresa of Avilla and Desmond Tutu tucked into the corners of your mind. But me? I carry around a sound bite from those famous spiritual giants, the TV-show characters Cagney and Lacey. It's true. I remember one episode in which Cagney needed to say good-bye to her daughter. She finally blurted, "It's not the letting go that hurts; it's the holding on."

The more we hold on to the known and imagine we can somehow stop time, the more our fear about the unknown future grows. The more tightly we grasp our lives, the more our sentimentality becomes cloying and holds everyone back. We treasure the known . . . treasure the known . . . treasure the known . . . Oops! . . . We worship the known.

But how do we let go and journey from the known to the unknown? Actually, the communion of saints showed us how. We can think back and recall how resurrection arrived in our congregations:

- For the stricken widow, we watched new life arrive during three years of painstaking grief, after which the roses came back into her cheeks and she returned to her quilting group.

- For the distraught parishioner, we saw new life appear as he laid out his problem in our office and walked out the door with a lighter load.
- For the youth group, a resurrected life dropped in somewhere between the time they left church as strangers on a school bus and a week later when they returned as a community united by a Habitat for Humanity building project.

We can also gain courage from the stories of other pastors who have stepped out in faith. Pastor Davis watched his parishioners face many endings and calls to embrace new life during his pastorate in a large congregation. Now he needed all their lessons. Pastor Davis had used his organizational and relational skills to advance to a position on a large church staff that included being responsible for pastoral care programs of the parish. But the more he managed congregation business, the farther he felt from the call that brought him to the ordained ministry in the first place. Determined to follow God's leading, Pastor Davis and his wife prayed about what to do and how to face new life. Slowly, as the weeks passed, their fears of upending their security were trumped by the fact that Pastor Davis' elderly father, who lived on the opposite coast from them, would soon need their assistance. Finally Davis' wife found a job opening in her field, working with an organization in the community where Pastor Davis' father lived. They made the move across the country with tears in their eyes and a sense of adventure in their hearts.

Pastor Davis wondered often on the cross-country trip what his new life would look like. Would he be called to another multiple-pastor staff? Would he feel as close to a new set of parishioners? In fact, the answers did not come soon. When he arrived in his new state, no calls came from congregations in his denomination, so Pastor Davis extended his job search. Eventually he landed a position as manager at a shelter where people spent hours each day sitting at tables, staying warm, playing cards, and talking to one another. Pastor Davis circulated among those tables, listening to stories of survival, offering his sense of humor, and being inspired by the tenacity of hope. As much as he was happy to lend an ear, Pastor Davis also looked forward to offering some tangible help—like a sandwich—that lit up people's faces. Every day at lunchtime, Pastor Davis staffed the counter where folks lined up for sandwiches and coffee. As he pulled one Styrofoam cup after another off the top of the stack and filled it with coffee to hand to a hungry person, he always thought of the Communion cups he used to distribute. "Blood of Christ, shed for you."

Coffee, foot powder, sandwiches, a smile—little by little Pastor Davis learned a smidgen of what folks who live on the streets need to survive. And in doing so, he discovered what his ministry needed for him to survive. New life. Not his own new life, as he had imagined. But the new life happening each day around him. Like the new life of a long-term client finally finding a place in temporary housing. Or the new life of a conversation with someone about how God looks from under the bridge. And the new life of a million pleases and thank-yous uttered with all sincerity. Pastor Davis never expected that the ones who showed him new life wouldn't even have an address. But then again, before Pastor Davis even had a name or address, God knew what to call him: "Beloved."

For Reflection . . .

1. What are you holding on to? Who could offer support to you in your letting-go process?
2. Were you a pastor who pushed for change in your congregation? How is your affinity for or fear of change affecting your departure?
3. What did kids and teenagers in your church model about change?

Down to the River to Pray

When we became pastors, perhaps we naively imagined we would always swim in the sweet waters of baptism. And we did swim in those lovely blue pools, floating on our backs and feeling God's spirit beneath us.

But we probably didn't realize when we made our ordination promises how often we would also swim in the polluted waters of sin, even in the church. Evil, as well as goodness, surrounded us during our pastorates. We felt it. At times we wondered if we could survive our own sin and others' flaws. Our sins, as well as the failure of others and an institution, accompany us out the door. How do we begin to face the unfinished business of our disappointments and disillusionment? Can we mend at least the edges of our brokenness? We're not even sure what was our fault and what was beyond our control.

As people of the book, we believe that biblical characters inform us on our faith journeys. One such character is Naaman, whose story we read in 2 Kings. When we first meet Naaman, he is truly inconsolable; in fact, he's afflicted with leprosy. Sores cover him; a cure evades him. While Naaman's

afflictions distinctly mark his body, our hurts are more likely
to hide inside. But like Naaman, we can go looking for a cure.
We can start by composing an honest "I'm sorry that . . ." list
that begins to identify our inner afflictions.

I'm sorry that . . .

I couldn't fix what was broken at church.
I wanted to be finished.
I didn't do more.
I couldn't stay forever.
I didn't take care of myself.
I couldn't reach out to other pastors.
I didn't ask for help.
I stayed too long.
I didn't appreciate what I had.
I dragged my family into the unknown.
I worshiped the church instead of the gospel.
I forgot to pray.
I resent my successor.
I was blind to my complicity with sin.
(Name your own)

The afflictions that ravage us include some sins that we need
to confess, some issues that we need to discuss, and some hurts
that we need to grieve. And most likely, all those categories
overlap. But the entirety of our afflictions, like all Naaman's
sores, ooze with hurt and need to be cleansed in holy waters.
The good news, we learn from Scripture, is that they can be.

> Elisha sent a messenger to [Naaman], saying, "Go, wash
> in the Jordan seven times, and your flesh shall be restored
> and you shall be clean." But Naaman became angry and

went away, saying, "I thought that for me he would surely come out, and stand and call on the name of the LORD his God, and would wave his hand over the spot, and cure the leprosy!" . . . But his servants approached and said to him, "Father, if the prophet had commanded you to do something difficult, would you not have done it? How much more, when all he said to you was, 'Wash, and be clean'?" So he went down and immersed himself seven times in the Jordan, according to the word of the man of God; his flesh was restored like the flesh of a young boy, and he was clean.

2 Kings 5:10–14

Our afflictions need to be cleansed—and we cling to God's promise: We will be made whole. Our baptism, our prayers, and our tears certainly help us to heal, of course, but we don't cure ourselves. Instead we risk following God's messenger to a place of healing, like Naaman finally did. God's helper advises that the cure is deceptively simple—just wash and trust. Again and again.

But where are these supposed messengers of God who want to lead us to healing waters? We feel all alone; we cannot see the guide right in front of our eyes. Naaman had the same problem. In his case, his ego needed downsizing before an unexpected servant of God could address his leprosy. Our blindness might have a different cause. As pastors, we spent our days around other people all the time. Now we may find ourselves alone, and isolation can do weird things to our minds. We can actually forget that we really don't have to bear all our own burdens and sort out our myriad feelings alone. In fact, with all due respect, we can't.

So where are these supposed messengers of God who want to lead us to healing waters? Closer than we think. Martin Luther recognized that *the saints* (people of faith blessed with the indwelling of God's Holy Spirit) serve as God's messengers on earth. Luther viewed as almost sacramental something he called the "mutual conversation and consolation of the saints." The saints of God stand in God's place to assure penitent sinners that they are forgiven in the sight of God. We offered that assurance as pastors. Every Sunday we spoke the words of absolution. Martin Luther reminds us that with or without a robe and collar, however, all Christians are called and empowered to confess our sins and receive absolution in the company of the saints—from members of new congregations, our spouses, close friends, spiritual directors, and former colleagues.

When we leave ministry, we carry all sorts of junk with us. Some we've had all along, some we acquired because of particular people or experiences . . . In our watery dips, we confess all that sin and hurt. Naaman didn't just go into the water, though. He was transformed. And in the end, we too are healed—absolved.

We may experience the deepest healing of all in the realization that we can still proclaim that gift of absolution to others. And so I proclaim it to you now, pastors. May you believe that you are already absolved, even as you dip and soak away your pain and loss.

For Reflection . . .

1. Which items on the "I'm sorry" list seem most pertinent for your healing experience?

2. Read more about Luther's concept of mutual conversation and consolation of the saints.
3. How can you support other clergy in their transitions?

Enough

"Here, would you hold this?" says a pastor who is leaving—to a church council, to another pastor, to God. "This" is the enormous responsibility of carrying a church—the tedious details, the relentless schedule, the countless people, the infinite needs. "Take this parish, please. I have brought it to you."

Enough—that's what we're celebrating at the time when our work is fulfilled and God's glory has carried us. Enough. Enough of God's grace to have fulfilled a call. Enough of God's strength poured out to have rounded the bend. Enough of God's people to see how faith works.

A backpacking trip once educated me about enough. After three days, two nights, six thousand feet of elevation gain, twenty-seven miles, one windstorm, twenty water stops, and one roll of duct tape to bandage the blisters on our feet, we neared Holden Village, the destination for our backpacking trip through the Cascade Mountains. Surely those last several miles would just evaporate, we thought. But we were kidding ourselves; each step had to be taken. When our minds leapt ahead and we tried to be at the end of the trail before we were there, the present hurt even more. With shaky knees, we hiked down the long descent and across the remaining miles of flatland. The trees thinned; we finally left the woods and entered the meadow. We drank up the music of the creek bubbling beside us.

Our spirits lightened as we encountered other hikers who were walking out from Holden. They carried only daypacks, so we knew when we saw them that we were getting close. More steps and more steps. Our growing giddiness and tired legs made us trip over roots on the trail. We began to see the signs that we were almost home free.

How to savor the arrival moments that we had imagined for all those miles? Notice, and pay attention, and give thanks. Across the final field we strode as our spread-out team of hikers gathered together to share the victory. With huge sighs and large grins, we dumped our backpacks at the sign for Holden Village. We got out our cameras for the celebration. Our sunburned, bug-bitten faces beamed. We did it! We had trekked and learned and suffered and bonded and pushed and thrown ourselves into God's world. We reached the goal that empowered us; we hugged and giggled and pounded one another on the back.

And we celebrated. What good is the land of milk and honey, after all, if you can't indulge in the melding of milk and honey—ice cream! We slurped down enormous double-dip cones with not one single sprinkle of guilt.

"Would you mind carrying this?" we wanted to say to strangers, as we looked at our dusty, trusty backpacks on the ground. We had carried those packs for twenty-seven miles across two mountain passes. We had tied our shoes and our hats and our dreams to the outsides of those packs. And now we couldn't even imagine once more hoisting our heavy loads onto our shoulders to carry them up a flight of stairs. We were finished; our bodies were light.

Could you carry this congregation for me? We are lightened by the satisfaction of bringing it home safely across a long journey. We carried this congregation up backbreaking switchbacks, ruined our knees on downhill skids, figured out how to find balance again and again and again as the load of a congregation shifted each day. Together with God's people, we were amazed on the trail—by the sights and the surprises and the drudgery and the songs that got us up the hills. Along the way we discovered God's enough. Enough forgiveness, Sunday school teachers, Communion wafers, poinsettias, words, water, dignity, prayers.

Now we can lay our heavy load, a congregation, at God's altar and give thanks for the experience. Thanks for the log bridges we somehow got across. Thanks for the clear, windy days that dried out the effects of the soaking nights. Thanks for the blueberries along the trail that slightly outnumbered the biting flies.

Thanks that we made the trip and that God brought us safely across.

Now we can stand up anew, unburdened, and raise our hands to God's enough.

When Jesus called Lazarus out from the tomb, Lazarus leapt from cold darkness to blinding warmth. We can celebrate new life with Lazarus. The *e* for the empty on which our spirits were running is now the first letter of God's *enough*, God's clear certainty that we are the humans who must live within limits, even as we push them and proclaim God's limitlessness. God carried us as we carried a congregation, and God carries us still. And the unknowns that we will face can't be any more challenging than the knowns of a congregation, can they?

Lazarus knew how to thank God for the light. He ran out of the tomb with the vestiges of the past streaming off behind him and celebrated the unbinding of all that had defined him as dead. In future days, we may run to pick up the bindings that fell off of us and try to reclothe ourselves with identity and purpose. But for now, and forever, we can give thanks for our lightness and for the Light.

For Reflection

1. What did you carry in your heavy satchel as a pastor?
2. Did you remember to go back and say thank you? If not, how about now?
3. What is your greatest relief about being finished?

Part 3

From Good-bye to Hello

Language Lessons

Make the H sound
Huh, huh, huh
As in henceforth, hopeful, hallowed, humble, heads up,
  and hemidemisemiquaver★
Now the L sound
LIIIIIIIIIIIIIIIIIIII
As in launch, listen, loom, lesson, livelihood, and
  luminescence
Finally, make the O sound
Oh, oh, oh
As in omnipotent, oblate, overflow, and
"Oh, no, my microphone is on."
Huh . . . llllll . . . oh
May it be so.

★a 64th note

Learning to Say Hello Again

The sshhhhhhhing of a bicycle chain slowing to a halt seeped through our screen door. Our language teacher, Moumini (moo-mee-nee), swung himself gracefully off his bicycle, his robes flowing behind him but somehow never soiled by the ride. Moumini adjusted his "African bicycle helmet," the small fez that Cameroonian men wear on the backs of their heads, and tapped a light rap on the door.

As we gazed out toward the bleached African sun, Moumini appeared to be a specter at our door. But a specter, as far as I know, does not call out "Toooo" (rhymes with yo, but the *o* is stretched out further).

Moumini creaked open the screen door and entered as we rose to shake hands, according to Cameroonian custom. A litany of questions, also known as African greetings, followed our handshakes: How are you? How are your cows? How are your crops? How are your children? How is your wife? The order of the greetings never changed; the responses never varied. Fine, fine, fine, fine, fine.

Yet Cameroonian greetings served as an important ritual for saying hello. And when we enter new territory, we need to learn how to say hello once again. After all the work we did as pastors to say good-bye and exit through a church door (remember?), and all the effort we put into not turning back, we now ask God to teach us to say hello so that we can enter new worlds.

Part of letting go of the congregations we've held so tightly is finding new handholds. It can take awhile to figure out what to grab onto. After all, our muscle memory is ingrained to our former churches. Our arms memorized exactly how far to reach to grab the edges of our old pulpit; our elbows learned just the angle with which to bend as we consecrated the elements at the altar.

After leaving and grieving, we now face the dilemma of teaching our muscles new patterns. Our gregarious personality may *push* us back out into the world. We're lonely, so we go looking for others. Or our Christian sense of mission may *pull* us out of our caves of privacy as we seek "the least of these" whom Jesus served. Or we might not be able to move at all. We might feel stuck in place—still grieving our dismemberment and uncertain about where to start afresh. Crossing new thresholds, especially new church thresholds, can feel as frightening to us as it must have felt to the strangers who entered our congregations for the first time.

Eventually—and this may take even longer than the months or years church councils sometimes need to enact change—life calls us to get out and learn to say hello again. Sounds pretty silly. We all know how to say hello, after all. Or not. Just like my husband and I needed to learn to say hello in a new way in Cameroon, all of us must learn new languages to enter unknown communities. While we're in the hello-learning process, we come up against our ignorance and awkwardness. But we find brothers and sisters in the faith willing to usher us in to fresh places.

Hellos require humility; we become the stranger who must reach out to others. Hellos uncover vulnerability; we neither know, nor control, the new systems into which we move. Hellos teach patience; we need time to figure out how an unfamiliar community will greet us.

Although Cameroonian greetings seemed perfunctory to me, they served a purpose. The greetings slowed people down and made them look one another in the eye. And of course hellos in Africa always came with a handshake. And a hand-shake is a handhold, *n'est ce pas*?

"Greet one another with a kiss," instructed Paul. He oper-ated in a North African culture and knew the importance of beginning our encounters with signs of hospitality. Paul made a big to-do about saying hello. In his letters he never launched into his message until he shared formal introductions. First, Paul invoked God's spirit and set the context of hello as recognition of our connection in Christ: "Grace to you and peace from God our Father and the Lord Jesus Christ" (Rom. 1:7). Subsequently, Paul honored others in his opening greetings by giving thanks for their ministry: "We must always give thanks to God for you, brothers and sisters, as is right, because your faith is growing abundantly, and the love of everyone of you for another is increasing" (2 Thess. 1:3).

I doubt if the extensive greetings that opened Paul's letters would fit in the first screen of a text message on our cell phones. In our day, we try to abridge our communications down to single lines delivered as quickly as possible. We often even dispense with the receiver's name at the beginning of our message. Perhaps warp-speed communication feels efficient, and brief messages might keep us on our offspring's radar. But in this chapter we're talking about hellos that stick longer than a text message.

Many essential and challenging hellos await us out in the world. Hellos to new congregations and communities and to a renewed sense of purpose. Hellos to our baptismal foundation, fresh phases of discipleship, and as-yet-unknown ways of experiencing God. These hellos deserve care and attention. Launching into new places is not easy! Will they welcome me? Will I prove useful? Will I find some of what I lost? All these questions churn around inside, and we begin the process of finding the answers with one word—Hello.

Abundance

On my first day in my first class at seminary, I was lucky enough to encounter Pastor Bob Leslie, who taught pastoral care. Bob drew on his decades of experience as a hospital chaplain to teach future pastors a simple way to invite grieving people to start talking about their losses. In his gentle-but-courageous manner, Bob Leslie merely sat down next to his companion and said, "Tell me about your loved one's death." With that clear invitation, Bob's companion would open up and talk about the event and its meaning.

Bob reiterated that most people really need to talk about the key experiences of loss in their lives and don't get enough chances to do so. He advised that we listen for the very first thing a person says in response to the invitation. That first statement usually encapsulates something essential about their loved one. Bob Leslie also recommended paying close attention to the things that came up again and again as a person talks about their loved one. Those are the issues that linger.

If Bob Leslie sat down next to each of us in his unhurried way and said, "Tell me about your pastorate," what would we say first? What would we talk about again and again? We may get few chances to talk about our truly unique lives as pastors or the challenges of letting go of that role.

Why do we need to talk about our ministries? Because our experiences, both positive and negative, grew out of our faith and shaped our faith. And our experiences, both negative and positive, can provide some clues that lead us to our next mission steps.

The very skills and passions that enabled us when we served as pastors are the skills and passions we can utilize as we search for new purpose. If our humor got us through tough conflicts at church, our humor can also ease some of our lonely days. If music girded our ministry, music can be the gift that will carry us into the future.

Consider these thumbnail sketches of pastors who will use their particular penchants to move into unknown futures:

Pastor Anne was more defined by the congregation and being a pastor than she imagined herself to be. She left with the deep satisfaction of knowing she did her best, but struggled with how to continue to serve the justice causes that energized her ministry. A lifetime of flexibility—many moves and international living—served to help her regroup and join new justice organizations.

Pastor Charlie was so natural at being a pastor that he would always retain his extroverted pastor personality. But he found letting go of the affirmation and leadership to be complicated. Pastor Charlie used his gift of humor to help him learn to be gentle with himself through the transition.

Pastor Gary came to terms long ago with his 100 percent identity as a pastor, and he chafed under other pastors' leadership when he tried to be a parishioner. His bishop helped him find a congregation that wanted to call a visiting pastor to bring Communion to homebound members.

Pastor Norma, a very maternal pastor, grieved retiring from the congregation like a parent grieves the empty nest. She gathered up her nurturing skills and took them with her to volunteer as a worship leader at a local church preschool.

As part of her tradition, *Pastor Liu* continued to serve as a beloved elder in her Chinese congregation. Evangelism always compelled her in ministry, and she will now have more time to lead Bible study and meet with prospective members.

If the kind and astute Bob Leslie sat next to us, and said, "Tell me about your pastorate," perhaps one of the last issues we would talk about, the issue that lingered for us, would be the issue of how to handle our abundance. We might not immediately recognize our riches, because we're so focused on our losses. But over time, if we pay attention to what bubbles up, we'll begin to realize that we're holding onto a great wealth of experience.

"Tell me about your abundance," Bob Leslie would say. And his invitation would tap a new vein of grace. Tell me about working with God's people to build communities of faith, about the privilege of being present at holy moments like worship, illnesses, decisions, crises, and deaths. Tell me how you've been blessed.

Pastor Olson sat for a decade in retirement with the stories of his ministry nipping at his memory. Finally, his grandchildren inspired him to share with them what he learned by getting out into God's bigger world. He wanted them to know the stories of his missionary adventures in Africa. So he spent a year writing a book. He cried and laughed and told his story so that his grandchildren could do the same. Pastor Olson's gratitude flowed out of a pen as he relived those years when he witnessed so much suffering and generosity. When he was finished, we carried his manuscript to a print shop, had it copied on nice paper and bound, and gave copies to his loved ones and others who might be interested. In so doing, Pastor Olson honored the story as well as the effort it took to write it all down.

Abundance can't be managed, controlled, or measured any more than the blessings and burdens of a pastor's life can be explained. But abundance longs to be poured out, as it was poured out onto us.

For Reflection ...

1. Martin Seligman, founder of the field of positive psychology, validated the idea that the skills and passions that enabled us as pastors can also work for us as we search for new purpose. Go to his website Authentic Happiness, http://www.authentichappiness.sas.upenn.edu, to find out more about evaluating your strengths. You can also utilize other strength finders—either free ones online or those available through an employee assistance counselor or other sources.

2. Write a thumbnail sketch of your pastoral personality, like the ones on page 88. What do you love that will help you adjust to new circumstances?

3. Imagine a beloved friend or family member asked you to share three of the most memorable days as a pastor. Write, draw, and muse about some experiences that stay with you.

Long Distance Call: Emmaus

On the day they walked to Emmaus, the followers of Jesus were preoccupied with a good-bye. They had no idea when they politely greeted the stranger who joined them on the road that by the end of the day, Jesus would turn their good-bye into a hello.

In spite of their deep sadness and wrenching confusion, Jesus's followers stepped away from the cross, found one another, and went for a walk. So full of faith in Jesus that his departure both clarified and unnerved them, they felt compelled to talk to others about what filled their hearts. Who else but other followers could begin to fathom their loss?

Why Emmaus? Perhaps they had to get home. Or they had to go somewhere—and why not Emmaus? Maybe the next day was market day in Emmaus, or they had friends in Emmaus to whom they wanted to tell their story. Who knows? So Jesus's followers departed . . . and so do we.

Emmaus proved the perfect distance from Jerusalem. The shock of Jesus's death gave these travelers all the strength they needed to walk ten kilometers. They barely noticed their feet, for Jesus's life story poured out of their lips. Jesus's death broke open their pain and their passion. All they could do was go back to the story and tell what happened to Jesus and to them.

Unselfconscious, unstoppable—the disciples delivered the story of Jesus to a stranger. The measure of the story's truth was their inability to keep it to themselves. This man on the road unwittingly reconnected the disciples to the holiness and purpose they feared they had lost. A nameless stranger cradled their grief, shouldered their emptiness, and drew them close to the God they knew.

We talk so much about being called *to* a holy place as pastors, but the call to depart is equally holy. And so we turn and walk away. Our job as pastors was always to tell Jesus's story. The church ordained us to Word and Sacrament ministry. We told Jesus's story on Sundays and Wednesdays, on retreats, and on our knees. But to whom will we tell our story now? Will treasured ministry companions listen to our experience of leaving a congregation? Who will walk with us for a couple of hours while we pour out the words, while our racing minds settle down, so that we can get ahead of the pain that dogs us, the fear puppies that nip at our heels. Who will receive our stories?

After standing at the cross of our losses, a new place calls us. The call might sound faint from over six miles away.

During the days, weeks, months, and even years between leaving one pastoral experience of serving Christ and finding another faith community where we will serve, whether as pastor or parishioner, we may be hard pressed to comprehend how God is working in our lives. We may be blinded to God's will for our lives. But God's love lives on for us in unimagined epilogues. God's people await us; new settings bless us.

The terrain between holy sites differs drastically from our dwelling in either location. We are in transit, like the disciples on the road to Emmaus. But God walks with us, even when we don't recognize God's company. God is leading us—way beyond our former congregation and the old wineskins.

Do we love the story of the Road to Emmaus because the story has a happy ending? No, we love the story because it has a joyful ending. Jesus restores the believers' faith that they are not alone. At Emmaus, Jesus returned in the familiar, the breaking of the bread that comforted and astounded them. God can always work through what we know and practice and treasure, Word and Sacrament. Because of Emmaus, we live in hope that God awaits us at the end of every road, each call, and the adventure known as life. God mysteriously accompanies us in ways we can't understand or imagine or predict. Eventually we see more than we saw, more than we would have seen if we had never taken that walk, if God hadn't died to us in one form and been raised in another. Eventually we run and tell again.

For Reflection . . .

1. Take a ten-kilometer (6.2-mile) walk with another pastor, and talk about what being God's servant has meant to you and means to you now.

2. Where did Jesus meet you on the road today? Write the story of your encounter. Try a travelogue style.
3. At what periods during your pastorate did you feel God was most absent? Most present?

Starting from Scratch

Pastor Rosa wandered around her kitchen, unable to focus. She had been retired for a few months now. The ennui of aimlessness and an uncertain path were setting in. Should she try to make peace with a life of leisure? After all, she loved having time to read the paper and work in the garden. But she felt restless and missed having a structure to her days. Who knew that she would still possess this much energy? She didn't miss the onerous duties of pastoring per se, but missed having something to do and someone to be. Pastor Rosa wandered into the kitchen. Her gaze fell on a stack of cookbooks on her kitchen shelf. She thumbed through a couple of cookbooks and found an idea. She would make tortillas from scratch. At least it was something familiar—and comforting—to do. She used to help her grandmother make them—while standing on a chair with a dishtowel tied around her chest—but she hadn't made tortillas since her beloved *Abuela* died while she was away at college. During her busy working years, she simply grabbed a package of tortillas at the grocery store. They tasted tough and papery, unlike the soft, fresh tortillas her grandmother used to make.

Rosa (we can drop the *Pastor* for now, as she is trying to do) began to mix the tortilla dough. Such a simple recipe: flour, baking powder, salt, shortening, water. She formed the round tortillas and patted them vigorously with her clapping hands. Onto the hot pan the tortillas went, one by one. Fry, flip, fry some more. As Rosa rhythmically cooked the tortillas, she wondered about whether she could create a simple recipe for moving on with her life. After all, she was starting from scratch too. Should her life recipe include three steps? Why not? Three points always worked for her sermons.

Rosa tasted first one, then another warm tortilla and stacked up the rest for later. She found her Bible and settled into a chair. How many weeks had gone by since she'd opened her Bible? Without a weekly sermon to write, she had lost this spiritual discipline. That might be part of her restlessness, she realized. Rosa thumbed through the Gospels, looking for stories of God's people starting from scratch, and quickly found the story of Jesus calling his disciples in the Gospel of John.

In John 1:35–42 Jesus's first words to his potential followers were a question: "What are you looking for?" Rosa read that question and in that moment felt Jesus there with her in her confusion and loss, caring for her and honestly wanting to know her answer.

What are you looking for? During Rosa's busy years of parish ministry, she was usually wrapped up in what her parishioners were looking for. She felt fulfilled enough as a pastor to sense that she had found satisfaction working with others to help them seek and do God's will. Now that her life had shifted, "What are you looking for?" sounded like a totally new question. "Truth be told, Jesus . . . I'm looking for you. I want to figure out how to be your disciple again."

In John's account, Jesus simply walked by as John the Baptist proclaimed, "Behold, the Lamb of God." Rosa thought, I used to be John the Baptist, pointing others toward Jesus. Now I'm looking for Jesus too. I want to trust him again, safe

in the coolness of his shadow, like the first disciples. Trust.
Rosa felt sure that was step 1 of her starting-from-scratch
recipe.

During the next weeks Rosa stayed busier. In fact,
she fried tortillas many afternoons. Being busy proved to
be a better alternative to feeling lonely and useless. But
Rosa recalled that when she served churches, *busy* didn't
necessarily mean "purposeful." She always hoped that the
life of her congregation would center around meaningful
mission rather than never-ending activities. Now that she
was retired, she didn't want her own life to merely revolve
around busyness.

Rosa continued to read and puzzle over John's account
of Jesus calling those first disciples. She wanted to know,
What happened next, after they trusted this new rabbi?
What was the next step in the starting-over recipe? "[Jesus]
said to them, 'Come and see.' They came and saw where he
was staying, and they remained with him that day" (John
1:39). Come and see, come and see. Of course. Come and
see where Jesus is staying, instead of focusing on where we're
stuck. Rosa felt her question to God shifting from "What do
want me to do now, God?" to "What are *you* doing God,
and how can I help?" Come and see. God was undoubtedly at work all around her, not merely in one congregation.
Keeping her eyes open for God at work seemed much more
refreshing than obsessing about her own life. Number one,
trust; number two, follow.

As Rosa's restlessness slowly ebbed, she began to think
back to the many community organization representatives
who spoke at her church when she was the leader. Surely she
could follow God to one of those charitable nonprofits now.

Of course she could simply go to a new congregation and get involved there, but Rosa wanted to find new worlds in which to serve.

Trust. Follow. Rosa took these steps with her on a personal retreat a month later, feeling hopeful that step three might show up there. She met with a spiritual director several times during the weekend and poured out her feelings about the emptiness of the transition.

"Do I sound pitifully needy?" Rosa worried. But the wise director looked straight at Rosa, thanked her for sharing her story, and assured Rosa, "Our lives don't belong to us alone. The things God teaches us are needed by the whole community." Rosa listened in startled silence. She hadn't really considered that her confused journey was valuable to others. Energized by the notion, Rosa shared more of her story with the supportive director. She talked about her starting-life-from-scratch recipe idea and her progress at finding new service opportunities. And then she tentatively offered her latest brainstorm: network with other retired women pastors to create a cadre of babysitters for the children of younger women pastors. They could be available to the younger pastors on Saturdays and during Holy Week and other busy seasons. "I could teach kids to make tortillas," Rosa laughed. In her laughter, she heard the last step of start-from-scratch. Trust, follow, share. She and God could take it from there.

For Reflection ...

1. What's cooking in your transitional life? Are you stewing, steaming, or studying? Write the recipe you've

been following. Is your recipe for transition working
for you?

2. Could you relate to Rosa's disconnection from the
   Bible since she left her parish? How are you tapping
   into the abundance of God's Word these days?

3. Cooking often includes balancing various flavors. How
   do you balance leisure and busyness? How do they
   contribute to your sense of purpose?

God's Temple

"Do you not know that you are God's temple and that
God's Spirit dwells in you?" (1 Cor. 3:16). That's an inspiring
slogan for a weight-loss campaign. Sadly, our bodies may have
inched toward temple size during our pastorates. Our bodies
expanded as we housed more and more confidences given
to us by our parishioners. We grew bigger and bigger as we
stuffed our dissenting opinions inside rather than expressing
our true thoughts. We never could quite figure out how to
disagree without being disagreeable, so we ate our words.

And then there was the weight of the world that we
carried as pastors. The worries about the Sunday offerings
that kept shrinking and the list of cancer patients that kept
growing, the concerns about a fraying church and a weeping
world. We tried to hold and carry so much, and our bodies
created more storage space to meet the task.

We also unconsciously puffed up, trying to appear as large
as the jobs we did our best to perform. When the disciples
ran into Jesus on the road to Emmaus, they did not recognize him. After we leave behind years of potluck dinners
and erratic schedules, we may look in the mirror and not

recognize ourselves either. That overtired, overweight pastor can't be me!

The shape many of us are in isn't terribly surprising. Yes, we pastors diligently exercised our spirits for the jobs we were called to do. We stretched and pummeled and built up our spiritual selves. They became strong and flexible enough that we could complete our own daily triathlons—the women's Bible study, followed by a strategy session with our building manager, followed by confirmation class. By the time we said good-bye to pastoring, our spiritual and intellectual muscles were toned by the laps we ran around the church year. To be sure, the body of Christ benefited from our spiritual strength. But *our bodies* may not have fared as well. For many of us, focusing on our spiritual selves became the perfect excuse for not exercising our bodies. At the end of our pastoring careers, we might have been able to touch the waters of baptism, but we couldn't touch our toes.

We pastors faced a particularly thorny challenge regarding physical fitness. Our temptation to merely focus on the spiritual, rather than the physical, proved very seductive. We worked at Souls-R-Us, after all. We operated on the "higher plane" of ideas about God and meaning, but sooner or later our too-heavy bodies grounded us, often in dire ways, like depression and hypertension and whacked-out blood sugar. Our robes were forgiving, shall we say, even if our physicians and health insurance companies were not. But when we stopped working sixty hours a week at church, we actually had time to pause in front of a mirror. And if a mirror is not as humbling a place to stand as a confession booth, I don't know what is.

For many of us, moving on means figuring out new ways of caring for our bodies. As we try to figure out, *How do I get from where I am to where I want to be?* we may remember the image of a great chasm that can't be crossed in the parable of Lazarus and the rich man. Unlike the characters in the Lazarus story, though, we can get from here to there—not by leaping, but by taking many little steps, enough new steps to reshape our body of Christ.

Try some of these steps:

1. Merely say hello to that person in the mirror. Greet that person with as much warmth as you would have greeted a visitor at the door to your church.

2. Write a letter to your body or a letter to God about your body. You might include a few familiar liturgical elements in the letter, like confession, forgiveness, and praise.

3. Get a dog or a pastor friend with whom to walk. Either way, you'll have a walking buddy!

4. Read *Women, Food, and God* by Geneen Roth, even if you're a man.

5. Get some new excuses. You're no longer at the mercy of an erratic parish schedule. Now you're going to have to find some new reasons why you can't move every day. Get creative about new excuses, or skip all that hiding and just start moving.

6. Surrender. Listen to music. Pretend the earth is a giant treadmill that helps us move. Set a timer for ten minutes. Do whatever it takes to stop thinking about why you can't or won't, and just take a step.

7. Practice consistent faithfulness. Parts of parish life are always changing, like people stopping in and crises piling up. But other aspects of congregations are consistent, like Sunday worship and monthly newsletters. Use the scheduling techniques that trained you to schedule daily exercise.

8. Be truthful: Is it hard to take care of yourself after you've taken care of so many other people? How can you make that shift?

As surely as alleluia came back after Lent, your endorphins and lighter spirit are going to kick in if you consistently say hello to your body. Practice what you preached—new life.

For Reflection . . .

1. What do you want your body to be able to do?
2. Whom do you talk to about changes in your body?
3. How could you simplify your routines to include more healthy choices?
4. Write an e-mail to your body every morning this week with the plan for the day.

Fifty-two Pews

Many Protestant churches strongly recommend that when you leave your pastor role, you leave your congregation. Your departure enables the next pastor to stand on his or her own rather than be eclipsed by your shadow. The separation can be hard, but it does force everyone to move on.

My husband and I knew that leaving our congregation would be a big loss for our daughters, because they were so at home there among people who loved them and had watched them grow up. Therefore, we dreamed up a creative family adventure for finding a new congregation. We decided to visit a new congregation each Sunday for a year and then pick one as our new home. We named our plan "Fifty-two Pews," and we amassed a list of congregations to visit from several denominations and faiths. God lives in lots of places—that's what we wanted our kids to see.

One of the things we discovered is that it's hard to go to a new congregation every Sunday. Locating the directions, getting the right time, figuring out where to park and where to sit (we all know about people having favorite pews!), and wondering whether strangers would welcome us seemed rather daunting at times. I remember the Sunday we drove across town to find out the church we planned to visit was celebrating an anniversary and had cancelled the first service. I remember walking into an African American church and wondering, "Is it *really* okay to be white and worship here?"

But we kept on visiting. The kids started to ask, "Where are we going this week?" We got to know our friends in a new way by asking them to invite us to their congregations. We visited a big-box church that offered seven services every Sunday and an out-of-the-box church with couches instead of pews. Countless parishioners warmly welcomed us and proudly told us about their congregations.

After attending each service, our family talked about the experience. The intention was never to judge the congregation—thumbs up or thumbs down—but to ask, "What did you notice?" Our kids noticed a wide range of things: They noticed that many of the men at the synagogue had comb-over hairdos. They noticed that there were security guards onstage at a young, hip church. They noticed when a lector got up, tapped the mike, and asked, "Is this on?" That would never have happened in our formal congregation!

The pile of bulletins, visitor postcards, and experiences grew for our family. We began to pay attention to bulletin boards; they spoke of what a congregation cared about. We began to alternate Sundays between the more familiar main-line Protestant churches, where we could easily identify the beginning, middle, and end of the liturgy—and the more unfamiliar congregations, where we experienced an altar call or tried to follow a Korean order of worship.

What did we learn? God is big! Our Sunday school kids sang it at my old church almost every Sunday. It's true—God resides in countless houses of worship. I'll never forget the look of relief on our daughters' faces when we arrived at Christmas Eve worship in yet another new church. The setting had changed, but the symbols remained familiar. A hundred tiny votive candles twinkled around the sanctuary, and we each received a candle to hold while we sang "Silent Night." The pastor preached about baby Jesus, and a liturgical dancer magically moved in the aisle. Our daughters' faces showed their relief. Jesus was born at this church too.

We wished more people would seek out opportunities to worship God in other congregations where they were not known by name. Jesus sent his disciples out to witness to the gospel, and they undoubtedly learned from strangers in each village along the way. Our experiences of welcome and displacement powerfully showed us how visitors could feel in our "home churches."

After our "Fifty-two Pews" experience of visiting congregations for a year, we joined a small church that felt like home. The commitment to join another congregation sat well with our whole family, so I was surprised to feel the leftover grief that popped up when we went through the new member process. Recommitting sealed the deal that the past was over. The reality of that change still stung, even as the step soothed us.

At first we felt very conscious about each unfamiliar action of Sunday morning—driving to a new place, going to new Sunday school rooms. One Sunday morning at our new church, the phone in the church office rang as I hustled around the office finding supplies for Sunday school. I unconsciously reached out to the answer the phone, but then I hesitated. I realized that I would not know the answers to most of a caller's questions. At my old church I had accumulated such a large store of knowledge that I could have answered the call and helped instantly.

Here are a few other things I noticed as a parishioner:

- I had to work more intentionally to get to know other parishioners. No one automatically knew my name.
- Getting used to the view from the pew, I caught myself panicking if my attention slipped during worship, because I was still programmed to be "on" during the service.
- I faced conscious choices about when and how to be involved at church. Because we pastors know

congregational life so well, we may be tempted in our
new church to get involved hither and yon—which is
fine, as long as we truly want to be involved, and we're
very clear that we're not the pastor.

- I unabashedly invited others to church. They didn't even
sniff the air anymore for an ulterior motive.
- I noticed my ego stung a bit on some Sundays as I
watched another pastor perform the rituals I loved
and reaping a special connection with a community of
believers.

After surviving the double whammy of surrendering congregational membership along with my job, now I can enjoy
the fruits of separating the two. I can go to church, not to
church/work. And now I am thrilled to have a relationship
with a real-live pastor of my own.

Throughout the process of leaving a call and moving
on, the only analogy I could come up with from the secular
world was the notion of remaking a family after death or
divorce. Family members are first tied to one family, then face
the confusion, grief, and awkwardness of leaving that family,
and finally move on to find a home in a new family, while still
being connected to the past. Transitions for blended families,
and pastors, can take time to heal, as we all try to adjust to a
new normal in a fresh home.

That's another thing we definitely found out: We considered our congregation our second home. I felt homesick
for my old parishioners—and the way the light streamed in
through the stained-glass windows. We felt church-homeless
until we settled again.

It's natural to make a church our home. We eat there and get cleaned up there. We have to figure out how to disagree there. We pass on our values across generations there. But the church is God's home, not just ours. And God is holding plenty of places at the table for the church-homeless whom, now more than ever, we can relate to and welcome.

For Reflection ...

1. Try a Fifty-two (or fewer) Pews experience of your own. Keep a journal about your reflections in unfamiliar places of worship. What surprised you? What did you resist? What did other pastors reveal to you about being a pastor?
2. What are the simplest gestures (like posting signs) a congregation can make to welcome visitors?
3. Some congregations join forces to address community needs; others become cloistered. How did forging relationships with other congregations enhance and challenge your community and ministry?

Going Back

Do you remember the ancient symbols for Matthew, Mark, Luke, and John? Early believers pictured the Gospel writers as an ox, a bird, a lion, and an angel. I didn't realize that the four little stained-glass windows next to the front door of my childhood church commemorated the Gospel writers. I didn't even realize that those windows still lived on in my memory until I went back to visit that congregation as an adult and

saw them again. Seeing those windows released a flood of
memories about growing up in that faith community. The
pew our family always populated awaited us, as did the very
same plastic flowers that graced Grace Lutheran's women's
bathroom when we were kids. Although much about the
church was exactly as I remembered it, not everything was
the same. We were welcomed back by the new pastor of the
congregation, which was now a Hispanic ministry. My parents
would have been glad that this congregation they helped to
build still thrived, but they would have wondered where old
friends had gone.

I visited my internship church a couple of decades after
I served there. "Will anyone remember me?" I wondered as I
returned to another congregation that had once been home.
I recognized several of my former church family's faces; their
smiles were seared into my mental scrapbook. I found out
that they remembered my smile as well. Our hugs hadn't lost
a single degree of warmth over the years, even if our faces
contained several more wrinkles. I looked around, somehow
expecting to see my internship supervisor, even though I knew
he was deceased. I did see several "children" I had taught on
internship; they were now tending to little ones of their own.

When I resigned after eight years in a pastoral call, I didn't
hang around to get in a new pastor's way. I stayed away rather
than confuse parishioners with my changed role. Staying away
forced me to grieve, and working through my sadness allowed
me to move forward with my life. Staying away proved to be
a healthy decision, but after a while I had no idea how to
go back either. I didn't know if anyone in that congregation
thought of me anymore, so I wanted to hide the fact that I still
needed them. Pride goeth before a call!

More than a year after we walked out the door of the church where I served eight years as a pastor, special friends invited us back there for their wedding. Our friends got married in the summer; so, as it turned out, the doors of the church were propped open. The church yawned open to welcome us . . . hmmmm . . . home? At least back.

I thought the relationships with former parishioners might have frayed with time, like the carpet. But as I crossed the threshold again, I could see that life continued in the parish, and many things were just the same as when I left. Yes, the bulletin boards had changed (and that didn't happen very often!); the entryway was freshly waxed. But my absence didn't silence the organ or the ministry. The narthex was not filled with cobwebs or with my ghost.

Some of the beloved parishioners were gone, having said hello to their own unfolding changes. But many who had served so faithfully while I was their pastor were still there, carrying out their callings in the congregation. Their "Welcome back!" went straight to a place in my heart that I thought was already healed. Our bonds were as strong as ever. But after the hugs and hellos, we all stood there awkwardly, as if we had once been married and were now pretending that we had only dated a couple of times. After all the intimacy of sermons and funerals and baptisms, after all the secrets that had been turned over to my care and that I still carried, we felt slightly uncomfortable. Our relationship had indeed changed. Going back teaches us that we might as well say hello to new places and people, because the past steps aside, even as God's story goes on. The greatest gift of going back is finding out that you can't.

For Reflection . . .

1. Trade sentimentality for a reality check: Make lists of what you honestly miss and don't miss about your former congregation.
2. Draw a picture of the door of your old church. Where are you in relation to that door?
3. Why do you think we feel so many emotions, often conflicting, about returning to our former churches?
4. Send a note to a former colleague sharing what it meant to you to serve together.

The Word Made Fleshy

Of all the pastoral duties she performed over her decades as a minister, Pastor Nancy loved baptizing babies most of all. She leaned on the hope of those baptismal mornings, when babies looked so formal in their fancy getups and parents seemed so earnest about making God a part of their family lives (at least temporarily). Nancy recalled the oily residue on her fingers, the heft of a chubby-legged baby on her arm, and the promise "I will, and I ask God to help me" on the sponsors' lips.

"Please welcome our new church family member," Nancy said each time she carried a newly baptized infant up and down the church aisles. Elderly women tipped up their heads to see the baby as Nancy passed. The women always reminded Nancy of nestlings, reaching up for morsels of reassurance that the family of faith would go on.

Pastor Nancy treasured baptism days, even when the babies squawked about their good news or when relationships among family members chilled liked baptismal water. No human foible could spoil the holy ritual; no imperfection could interfere with the welcome, belonging, and call of baptism.

Pastor Nancy respected the holy rite of baptism, so she felt a wave of poignancy when she saw the symbol of a baptismal shell on the cover of the good-bye card her colleague handed her. Inside the card he had scrawled these words: "May you always trust that your baptismal call came before your pastoral call." A rush of goodwill rose in Nancy when she read those words. Perhaps she wasn't severing her ties to God's work after all by leaving parish ministry. She knew that to be true from a rational perspective, but she still wondered how God felt about her impending departure.

Her colleague's words had reassured and grounded Pastor Nancy when she first read them. Months later, when the sting of leaving didn't feel quite so acute, she sat down one evening to reread her good-bye cards and was surprised to find she was receiving their messages and good wishes with new insights. This time around, her colleague's words piqued her interest about her baptismal call. What had been promised for her so long ago? Nancy pulled out her hymnal to find the baptism prayers and vows.

As she opened the hymnal, a lacy, crocheted cross bookmark fell out. Nancy picked it up and ran her finger across the rows of fine cotton loops. Her grandmother had given her that bookmark decades ago when she left to be a short-term missionary in Papua New Guinea.

Nancy instantly recalled a day long ago when she stood out on a mountain road in Papua New Guinea after spending the weekend with friends, hoping that the driver of the country bus would see her there, stop to pick her up, and take her back to the small town where she lived and worked. Nancy shivered, from both the chill of the morning air and the thought of being alone again. She dreaded her reintroduction to a culture that still felt confusing and alien.

The country bus careened around a curve, and the driver somehow saw her. She pulled herself up the stairs of the bus. As soon as it started up again, so did the comments of the drunken guys in the back seat. Their voices and laughter rose as they delivered sloshy, lurid opinions about foreign women. "Here we go again," Nancy thought, weary yet still intimidated by this harassment. She blinked back tears and tried to look calm.

Across the aisle from her, two robust market ladies listened for a while to all the rude comments, then motioned for Nancy to come and sit with them. They made a little space between themselves and placed her there. The cushion of God's love felt like soft fleshy arms. Those women gave Nancy a gift she never forgot. Of course they gave her protection. But the even greater gift they bestowed on her was the gift of belonging. Up until then, she still felt lost in their culture, but they showed her why she needed to give Papua New Guinea a chance.

Along with our livelihood, expertise, relationships, and status, we lose a sense of belonging when we step away from the known culture of our congregation. Nancy knew that now, and she realized that what she longed for was to belong to a community of faith again. Her eyes fell on the words in her hymnal about baptism:

God, who is rich in mercy and love, gives us a new birth into a living hope through the sacrament of baptism. By water and the Word, God delivers us from sin and death and raises us to new life in Jesus Christ. We are united with all the baptized in the one body of Christ, anointed with the gift of the Holy Spirit, and joined in God's mission for the life of the world.[3]

Nancy carefully wrote out the words, phrase for phrase, searching for clues in God's promises about where to go next on her baptismal journey:

A new birth into a living hope—Nancy thought that sounded like she was definitely going to begin again, yet where was unclear. Hope does not come with an address.

Delivers us from sin and death—Nancy thought about all the natural limits of parish life, like weekly deadlines and Sunday worship, that she had never really noticed but now missed. She asked God for liberation from the too-much freedom that had descended on her.

Raises us to new life in Jesus Christ—Whatever that new life might turn out to look like, Jesus would be the steady certainty.

United in one body of Christ—Aha! Evidently this baptism business dwarfed a single congregation. We're tied to a much larger community of faith, so large that we can never leave it.

Anointed with the gift of the Holy Spirit—Pastor Nancy always loved putting on her robe and sharing Sunday worship with her people. She always felt special in that robe, but now she remembered the cross she wore in oil on her forehead was as much a part of her specialness as her robe.

Joined in God's mission—Dang! She never could get that right. Ever since she left her parish, Nancy had reverted to thinking that her pastorate belonged to her rather than to God. The words reminded her that she shared ownership of a call with multiple generations, and lay and clergy alike.

For the life of the world—Long ago, an encounter on the other side of the world taught Nancy about belonging. She wondered now, even in her own displacement: Who needs to be welcomed?

For Reflection . . .

1. Write a letter to your baptismal sponsors about your faith journey.
2. What have you learned about belonging, both from within and from outside a congregation? Where do you belong now?
3. What strangers did you authentically welcome as a pastor?

Built for Giving

"The moving walkway is ending. Please look down," the airport voice warns us as we step off the conveyer belt. Even after hearing the cautionary words, we still feel the awkward shift from movement to stillness. We fall slightly forward as we cross that line from the moving walkway to the nonmoving floor. We can't simply stop our momentum in a trice. According to Newton's first law of motion, an object will continue moving at its current velocity until some force causes its speed or direction to change.

Where was the warning voice when we stepped out the door of the church? Why did no one alert us, "The constant busyness of parish life is ending; please look down"?

Learning to say hello to new ventures often includes saying hello to an altered pace. Stepping off the relentless conveyer belt of church calendars and pastoral demands can be great news. We may find a more natural pace once again and honor sleep, nutrition, and exercise. We walked a long time to get to the end of this walkway. Now we see a vision of places ahead we want to reach, at our own pace.

Learning to say hello also involves finding others who are willing to catch us when the walkway of parish life ends and we lurch forward, feeling awkward and unbalanced. It's never easy to be caught nor to receive help. We pastors are notoriously comfortable being the givers. After all, it's our job. We were built for giving. Why would we have become pastors if we did not want to give our lives to others? Joyfully some days, tediously others . . . but steadily giving. We passed out the morsels of liturgy, the chunks of bread at communion, the portions of prayer. But when we stepped off the pastor purpose machine, suddenly no one asked us the date of the next church council meeting or which prayer of the day to use or where we line up for the procession. God built us for giving. So becoming receivers can be uncomfortable.

But if we allow ourselves be receivers, we don't have to face the end of all our changes by ourselves. Awaiting us is a support system of caregivers who would like to catch us and help us learn to say hello to new possibilities and opportunities.

Spiritual directors, retired pastor colleagues, and nonclergy are just waiting to hear what we have to say. But what if we seem too needy? The truth is, we *are* needy. We've lost something huge, and the feelings about that loss are equally huge. There's shock at a new way of life that includes issues of grief, identity, imagination, letting go, satisfaction, regret, and transition. Sharing what's going on inside us is not an act of weakness but an act of courage.

We are built for giving, so we might be most surprised by the ones who give to us. We find ourselves hanging around longer at the grocery checkout counter, happy to have someone to talk to. We begin to discover that community comes in many shapes and sizes, including friends in a swimming-pool locker room, a group of moms at preschool, and the guys at the barbershop. We begin to value these chance encounters more deeply, begin to notice ourselves actually talking to people and getting to know them when we don't have to rush off.

Still, we were built for giving. So we can keep giving!

We give thanks for what has been, even as we can't imagine where we'll be without our old familiar role.

We give prayers for a universe of need, of which our own need makes us more aware.

We give a call to someone who can help us find our balance again after we stop moving so fast.

We give a chuckle about some of the silly things we gave as pastors.

We give God an opportunity to be the giver again.

At the end of the moving walkway called church, we find out what God is made of. We were built for giving; God is built forgiving. God forgives our stumbling, our denial, our confusion, and our decision to stop. God invites us to teeter, to stop, and to receive the wisdom of others about how to start again.

For Reflection . . .

1. Write about three things you received during the pastorate you are now leaving.
2. What has it been like for you to say hello to a different pace?
3. Where is God in all this?

God Stays

Pink flip-flops, blue crocs, tennies, sandals—a couple dozen pairs of shoes, shucked off onto the tile veranda. Precisely because God turned my shoes around, and I had walked away from a congregation years before, I could take my shoes off again and add them to this pile. I could walk into a home halfway around the world and share Bible study with two dozen members of a congregation in Indonesia.

The journey away from one particular, beloved congregation sometimes felt interminable, like the flights from the United States to Jakarta. But at least during those long, transcontinental airplane rides, I always knew my destination. On my journey out of a congregation, I merely headed off into the unknown. I didn't understand where to land next, so I tried lots of options and made some mistakes. I missed my church people and my pastor identity. I longed to belong to a faith community again and mourned the special connections that happen when fellowships serve God together. Just as I feared would happen on my way out of a church, I lost community and purpose. I didn't feel content until God led me to both again. God helped me endure the lingering pain and aimless confusion that eventually ended in new opportunities and endeavors,

> . . . like sitting in fifty-two pews as our family searched for a new church home,
> . . . like being blessed by an opportunity to serve as a chaplain in a cancer center,
> . . . like substituting for my pastor when she went on a three-month sabbatical,
> . . . like being a volunteer pastor in Indonesia and realizing a family dream of bringing our daughters on a mission trip.

If I hadn't had the courage to walk out a door, I would not have walked into an open-air church in Indonesia that didn't even have a door. I wouldn't have been surprised to feel so alive in the midst of vibrant Christians and faithful Hindus. For all the foot-dragging it took me to leave, and all the missteps after I left, God kept walking with me.

When I saw that pile of shoes outside the door in Indonesia, I saw a bigger picture. The reason I could say good-bye to a special group of God's people was that God stayed with them in the place where I once worshiped and served. I could meet and care for new members of the body of Christ, because God never stopped carrying the folks to whom I said good-bye. In fact it was God, not me, who was carrying them the whole time.

God stayed in the place I left, and God remained with me too. God accompanied me to a new place, even as God kept on loving the former place. How does God do that? Watch your shoes. You'll see.

For Reflection . . .

1. When was the last time you visited a new congregation? What did you learn about your community by attending another place of worship?
2. Where would you like to go on your next sabbatical, if you could go anywhere?
3. As you look back, what are some of the ways God has surprised you on your faith journey?

NOTES

1. Kathleen Norris, *Dakota: A Spiritual Geography* (Boston: Houghton Mifflin Harcourt, 2001), 11.
2. Roy M. Oswald, James M. Heath, and Ann W. Heath, *Beginning Ministry Together: The Alban Handbook for Clergy Transitions* (Herndon, VA: Alban Institute, 2003), 98–101.
3. *Evangelical Lutheran Worship,* 227

Hookdale
Trinity - Belleville
St Paul - Belleville
 Christ - Belleville
Maeystown
Hecker

St Paul Giles ᴼᴺᴬ
Trinity - affton ᴼᴺᴬ
UCC - affton
Fairview Heights UCC ᴼᴺᴬ
 St J. Granite City
St Peters - Ferguson
Epiphany ᴼᴺᴬ
Valmeyer
Brighton UCC ᴼᴺᴬ

ELCA Columbia
DOC Affton ᴼᴺᴬ
Christ Church - Cathedral